Dear
Mr. Jefferson

The garden gate with sentinel sassafras trees.

Dear Mr. Jefferson

LETTERS FROM
A
NANTUCKET GARDENER

LAURA SIMON

Crown Publishers, Inc.
New York

Published by Crown Publishers, Inc., 201 East 50th Street, New York, New York 10022.
Member of the Crown Publishing Group.

Random House, Inc. New York, Toronto, London, Sydney, Auckland
www.randomhouse.com/

CROWN and colophon are trademarks of Crown Publishers, Inc.

Printed in the United States of America

Library of Congress Cataloging-in-Publication Data

Simon, Laura
    Dear Mr. Jefferson : letters from a Nantucket gardener / Laura Simon. — 1st ed.
p. cm.
1. Gardening—Massachusetts—Nantucket.   2. Gardening—Virginia.   3. Monticello
(Va.).   4. Jefferson, Thomas, 1743–1826.   5. Imaginary letters.   I. Title.

SB453.2.M4S55   1998

635—dc21   97-27439

                                                                                      CIP

ISBN 0-609-60097-4

10 9 8 7 6 5 4 3 2 1

First Edition

Acknowledgments

Just as every garden blooms from the collected experience of many gardeners, every book grows from the wisdom and support of many people. For *Dear Mr. Jefferson* I am particularly indebted to an extraordinary group.

I offer wholehearted thanks to Meg Ruley, my agent, whose enthusiasm and belief were boundless and unwavering from the very first moment, even, I might add, when my own flagged. Similarly, I am grateful to Karen Rinaldi, my editor, for her exuberant embrace of my book, my garden, my dogs, cats, chickens, and ducks, and of Jimmy's honey, if not, yet, of his bees. And to Roy Finamore, who moves in mysterious but deliberate ways.

My thanks to Keith Crotz of The American Botanist, who always had the answer or else knew who did. To Scott Kunst of Old House Gardens, Jim Nau at the Ball Seed Co., Steve Garrison at Rutgers University, Janet Jones at the Nantucket Conservation Foundation, Mary Lethbridge of The Nantucket Tree Fund, and Steve Slosek at Moor's End Farm, who grows the best sweet corn I've ever eaten. And always to Deanna Slayton Avery, a.k.a. Dede, for her many years of gardening help and advice.

Ever willing and patient with technical assistance were computer whiz Mike Jones, superb copy editor Nancy Stabile, and good friend Tom Congdon, who talked me through my hyphen hysteria.

The best help of all came, as it always does, from my family. From my sister, Susan, whose faith in me is as wonderful as her food. From Roger, Homer, Jack, and Olive, comforting companions, all of them. And from my dear Jimmy. He keeps me going.

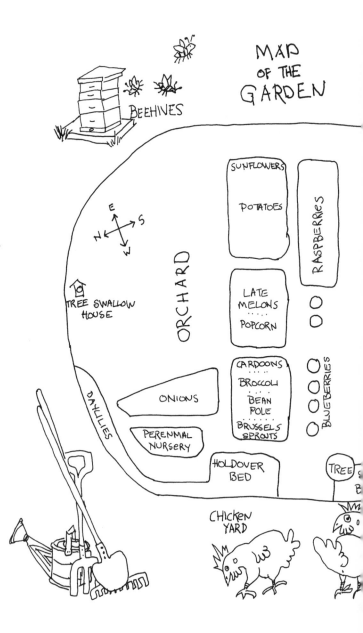

MAP
OF THE
GARDEN

BEEHIVES

SUNFLOWERS

POTATOES

RASPBERRIES

E
N
S
W

ORCHARD

TREE SWALLOW
HOUSE

LATE
MELONS
. . . . .
POPCORN

CARDOONS
. . . . .
BROCCOLI
. . . . .
BEAN
POLE
. . . . . .
BRUSSELS
SPROUTS

DAHLILIES

ONIONS

PERENNIAL
NURSERY

BLUEBERRIES

HOLDOVER
BED

TREE
B

CHICKEN
YARD

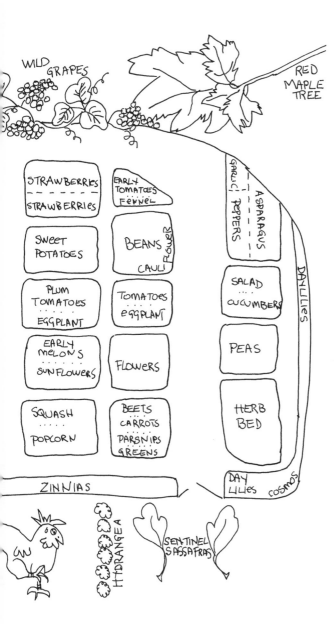

WILD GRAPES

RED MAPLE TREE

GARLIC PEPPERS

ASPARAGUS

DAYLILIES

| STRAWBERRIES | EARLY TOMATOES |
| STRAWBERRIES | FENNEL |

| SWEET POTATOES | BEANS |
| | CAULI |

FLOWER

| PLUM TOMATOES | TOMATOES |
| EGGPLANT | EGGPLANT |

SALAD
CUCUMBERS

| EARLY MELONS | FLOWERS |
| SUNFLOWERS | |

PEAS

SQUASH	BEETS
	CARROTS
POPCORN	PARSNIPS
	GREENS

HERB BED

ZINNIAS

DAY LILIES   COSMOS

HYDRANGEA

SENTINEL SASSAFRAS

For Jimmy

Mirabilis longiflora
Sweet Scented Four O'Clock
at around 7 p.m.

Introduction

I'll admit it's a bit of a conceit, this business of writing letters to Thomas Jefferson, but it's not as capricious as it sounds. Quite the contrary, it is the result of an eminently reasonable series of thoughts, each one coming on the heels of its predecessor in a wholly logical succession. Nor was this a lightning process, but grew rather like the garden itself, germinating from a single seed and slowly, eventually, bearing fruit.

In the very beginning, I was simply seeking a means of communication, a way of expressing the gardening thrall I'd suddenly found myself in. I wanted to talk shop, to discuss soil tilth and tillage, to compare varieties of carrots, and to analyze the relative merits of manure. I wanted to brag about getting rosemary seeds to sprout, a notoriously difficult feat, and to bemoan my continuing bad luck with the seeds of cleome. I wanted to rhapsodize about the sublime anticipation of winter planning and spring planting, to report on the great triumphs, and crushing disappointments, of summer. No question about it, my comments and observations had outgrown my gardening calendar and clipboards of lists and were similarly overfilling the spiral-bound notepad I'd added on as an auxiliary measure.

Jimmy, to whom I always turn first, wasn't the answer for this one. Of course, he still helps me prepare the beds every April and May and still takes a proprietary interest in the melons. He still whips up potting soil in his old yellow cement mixer, still suckers the tomatoes and drives stakes for their cages. But of late his attention has wandered away from vegetables and flowers to his newfound fascination with bees. Now his conversation runs more to supersedure cells and royal jelly than to the method of choice for mulching.

My sister, Susan, a cookbook writer and caterer in New York City, is understandably more interested in sampling the final harvest than in kicking around the arcanum involved in getting there, her charming terrace garden not withstanding. Roger, a gentlemanly, mostly Border collie, and Homer, a mostly comic, half pointer, will listen to me expound, riveted, as long as I hold Milk-Bones in my hand. As for Jack and Olive, big gray and little calico cats, respectively, not even bribery will prevent them from falling asleep or walking off as the mood takes them, although I will say that Jack enjoys sitting next to me in the garden, and that's something, if not precisely the confrere I sought.

I brooded about this at some length before it occurred to me that the solution to my problem was staring me in the face. I was a writer. I could *write* about my garden. After all, wasn't I doing just that already? But instead of the grime-smudged notes I'd been squeezing into the calendar margins, I could stick a sheet of paper into the typewriter and discourse in whole sentences and full paragraphs, just as if I were writing one of my books. The decision to write letters followed so swiftly and certainly, I never thought about it twice. For one thing, I was still seeking the camaraderie of a good chat, but for another thing, there was a precedent.

In my younger years, before there was E-mail or fax, back when long-distance calls were an occasion and those overseas had to be booked in advance, I was a prolific letter writer.

During those years, Susan and I lived in Italy, though we ranged all over Europe and down through Africa to the Indian Ocean as well. My Smith-Corona, a nineteen-pound "portable," went everywhere with me, and long, ecstatic missives full of tropical lagoons and Middle Eastern souks were hammered out.

It had been several decades since I'd written one of those letters, but the time seemed right to start again. Maybe now there were fiber optics, maybe now it was as simple to converse with a friend in New Delhi as with the neighbor next door, but a telephone call can't replace the singular pleasure of a letter. It can't conjure images, or be tucked into a pocket to be reread later and savored again. No matter how high the technology, a phone can't carry the voice of the caller as distinctly as does a letter, which depends, for transmission, on something far more advanced than any wire or chip. A letter relies on imagination. That of the receiver as well as of the sender.

Besides, my last epistolary period had been marked by a recurrent theme. Travel. In those years I'd been intoxicated with travel. I relished the voyage, I reveled in the destination, I loved discovering new cultures and penetrating new languages, I loved tracking down and memorizing new flavors and smells. I even enjoyed the inevitable stretches of boredom.

Hmmm. Take away the T word, add twenty-five years, and I could be talking about gardening. New culture, new language, new flavors and smells. They have a lot in common, travel and gardening, not the least of which is my zeal for both. Which is why I never for a moment questioned my decision to write letters. They had worked for me once, and I was confident they would again. As I said, there was a precedent.

But after coming, happily, to this conclusion, I hit a roadblock on the next step. Whether in person or by post, I still needed someone to address. Granted, my field of possibilities had broadened considerably, now that I was no longer limited by proximity, but it didn't seem to be broad enough. I went around for weeks, more like months, trying out prospective addressees in my head. No one was right. My initial elation dwindled to nothing and disappeared.

In fact, the more I thought about it, the sillier I felt. It was a dumb idea. Contrived. In the rush of enthusiasm that had accompanied this would-be antidote to my gardening loneliness, I'd overlooked an important point. That group of travel letters I'd been holding up as a model had been written more to keep in touch with the people back home, especially my parents, than to unburden my soul. "Dear Hilda and Robert" had been the primary purpose, not the transported text that followed. The audience hadn't been an afterthought, I was beginning to realize. It had been the reason for the act. Subdued, I laid the letter idea to rest.

What happened next happened independently of this whole debacle and sometime after it had slipped my mind. It started with an idle thought on a January evening, an evening that was in no way unusual for Nantucket in the winter, being bleak and raw with the wind yowling off the Atlantic Ocean. Nor was the thought more than a mere flick, at first.

I was sitting, as I often am on such evenings, hard by the woodstove, my feet buried beneath a dog, a stack of seed catalogs at my side. When the thought occurred, I was thumbing through a catalog from a company called Totally Tomatoes, rather new on the market and boasting a startling two hundred and seventy-nine varieties of tomatoes. The first one was called

'Abraham Lincoln'. A hundred and fifty varieties later there was a 'Jeff Davis'. Several minor celebrities and a saint were listed in between.

Why wasn't there a 'Thomas Jefferson'? I wondered. After all, went my musing, popular history has it that he brought the tomato to America. That it was Thomas Jefferson who, at the dawn of our republic, convinced his fellow countrymen that tomatoes weren't poisonous. Even if this folklore isn't as entrenched in our national consciousness as, say, George Washington and the cherry tree or Theodore Roosevelt and the Teddy bear, surely Thomas Jefferson is more deserving of having a tomato named after him than either Lincoln or Davis. That was my thought and it vanished as rapidly as it had arrived.

Like so much else in my mind, though, this thought wasn't gone for good. It was simply lurking behind more immediate matters, like supper, waiting to pop out at the appropriate moment. That moment came several weeks later when my seed packets were delivered with the mail. As I held the envelopes of 'Jet Star' and 'German Strawberry', 'San Remo' and 'Brandywine', trying to imagine, as if by osmosis, what pleasures were in store for me six months hence, the thought returned.

Why wasn't I fingering a packet of 'Thomas Jefferson' seeds? Why wasn't I speculating about the sun-ripened flavor of a glossy red fruit named for the Founding Father of Tomato Cultivation? Then another thought struck me. What if Thomas Jefferson wasn't, in fact, responsible for promoting tomato consumption? What if this charming snippet of American mythology was just that, a myth? Or what if it wasn't even a myth? What if it was just a case of information being misfiled in my brain?

It still being winter, with few gardening demands, I resolved to track down the truth about the tomato. I started in my own library, an eclectic mix of classic encyclopedias, turn-of-the-century seed catalogs, and single-subject treatises, my most favorite being the 1886 *Sweet Potato Culture*. I quickly moved on to the Nantucket Atheneum and then, as soon as I was able, to the Massachusetts Horticultural Society Library.

I'll use any excuse to stop there when I'm in Boston. From the heavy wooden balustrades surrounding the mezzanine stacks to the sibilant sliding of oak card-catalog drawers to the unmistakable scent of masses of books, some old and musty, some acid-sharp new, the room bespeaks library. Not so large as to be overwhelming, nor so small as to seem incidental, and unapologetically, luxuriously, exclusively devoted to horticultural literature. Dignified and hushed, it is a genteel haven, especially in winter, from the clamorous, gusty street below.

It also has answers. In this particular instance, the answer was confirmations of both the long-standing myth and my new suspicions of it. The history of the tomato, it turns out, is a bit hazy, which has left it open for embroidery and outright invention. Its botanical birthplace, pinpointed only a few decades ago, was the coastal highlands of Ecuador, Peru, and Chile. How it found its way farther north, to be "discovered" and transported home by conquistadors, remains a mystery. Even cloudier is the account of its reintroduction and acceptance in North America, although there are more versions of the events than there are varieties of tomatoes.

The only consensus is that the seeds retraversed the ocean, arriving here from Europe. After that, the stories abound. Thomas Jefferson is a prominent figure in many of them, but against hard evidence to the contrary, the first instance of a tomato being eaten on these shores is most frequently attributed to an eccentric retired colonel named Robert Gibbon Johnson. In 1820 he is reputed to have consumed a bucket of tomatoes, standing on the steps of the Salem, New Jersey, courthouse, while hundreds of open-mouthed spectators waited for him to tumble down dead at their feet.

Despite the theatricality of this version, which is, by the way, reenacted annually in Salem, its historical veracity is in serious doubt. Moreover, what *is* well documented, and in Thomas Jefferson's own handwriting, in his own garden diaries, is the fact that he was growing tomatoes as early as 1809, although it wasn't until July 21, 1813, that he specifically mentioned making a meal of them. Still, that's seven years ahead of Colonel Johnson's alleged performance.

In addition, there's reason to believe that a substantial *forty* years previous, Thomas Jefferson was given tomato seeds to try by an Italian friend named Philip Mazzei. And by the 1780s, they say, he was sending them from Paris to western Virginia, where Robert Rutherford not only cultivated tomatoes with enthusiasm, he also devoured them when ripe and sang their praises to everyone in the district. In 1819, still in advance of Colonel Johnson's feat, tomato lore has Thomas Jefferson astounding a young girl in Lynchburg, Virginia, by eating a tomato over her front-yard fence.

In the course of my research, I came across enough references to Thomas Jefferson and tomatoes to make my initial indignation seem warranted. Although he may not have been the only early champion of tomatoes, he was certainly one of the most influential and, unquestionably, deserving of having a tomato named in his honor. The real discovery, though, was that he was deserving of having so many more vegetables and flowers and trees named in his honor. The phrase "avid gardener" scarcely did him justice.

"[T]here is not a sprig of grass that shoots uninteresting to me," he once wrote to his daughter Martha. It didn't take me much reading to realize that wasn't an insincere boast or just a pretty turn of words. There wasn't anything that grew that didn't seem to fascinate him. And tempt him to try it at Monticello, his mountaintop plantation a few miles south of Charlottesville, Virginia.

It was his pursuit of that temptation, though, that took my breath away. How in the days, long before mail-order nursery catalogs, or even reliable mail, he corresponded with friends and acquaintances all over the fledgling United States and throughout Europe as well, exhorting them to send him saplings and seeds and roots. How he dispatched his secretary, Meriwether Lewis, on an expedition into the vast, unknown West. Lewis's mission, undertaken with William Clark—to observe the natural and to bring back botanical specimens— may well be the ultimate plant order.

It went on. How he imported grapes from Italy. And the vintners to go with them. Along with broccoli and eggplant and radicchio. Radicchio! How he coddled French figs, sent to Mexico for peppers, and filled an eighteen-acre grove with dozens of kinds of trees.

By the time I discovered he planted sesame every year, in order to press the seeds for their oil, I knew I was reading about a genuinely inspired gardener. And while I can admire an illustrious statesman, and even venerate a creator of the concept of democracy, I can really relate to a gardener. As the accounts mounted—the mouldboard he invented for side hill plowing, for instance, or the radical philosophy of crop rotation he espoused—Thomas Jefferson gradually became more than a famous name in history, more than a Charles Willson Peale portrait hanging in a museum.

The face in the painting took on flesh with fair skin that burned and peeled "on exposure to the sun . . . giving it a tattered appearance," as his grandson described it. He suddenly seemed so real. It was easy to imagine him at Monticello, striding, stooping, examining, just like anyone else, suffering sunburn for the sake of his 'Tennis Ball' lettuce or his sugar maple experiment.

It was easy, too, to imagine a real voice behind his volumes of letters. I could all but hear the swift change in his tone as he wrote to George Washington, ". . . I put away this disgusting dish of old fragments, and talk to you of my peas and clover." As I could almost hear the sweet longing of an absent father when he wrote, one June day, to his daughter Maria, from New York, "We had not peas nor strawberries here till the 8th day of this month. On the same day I heard the first whip-poor-will whistle . . . and when had you peas, strawberries, and whip-poor-wills?"

It was somewhere around this time that I began to hear my own voice, tossing small remarks his way. In the third person, of course. After all, I wasn't crazy.

"Wouldn't Thomas Jefferson have enjoyed these," I might say when the first tulips bloomed. Or the peonies or the snapdragons or the heliotrope. "[A] delicious flower," he called it, "the smell rewards the care."

Or, "I'll bet this would have wowed Thomas Jefferson," I would find myself musing, as I laid out lengths of soaker hose. Or set grow lights over my seedlings. Or unrolled IRT mulch to warm up the sweet potato bed.

This casual commentary took an abrupt turn when I read about a trip he'd made to Italy from Marseilles. A trip made not on a comfortable train, overnight, as I have done, but in "about three weeks." A trip whose sole purpose was to unmask the secret of Piedmont rice, a rice deemed superior to that of Carolina, especially when prepared "au gras." A trip that led him, in the end, through Piedmont to Lombardy, where he filled his pockets (fashionably voluminous, fortunately) with what I can only suppose to be arborio rice. With cold-blooded calm, he slipped it back over the border to France and then sent it on to America, a deed so daring in 1787 that had he been caught in the act, he would have been put to death.

Whew! What a guy, I thought, remembering the gastronomic excursions Susan and I had set out upon when we were living in Italy nearly two hundred years later. Invariably, a steaming plate of risotto lay at the end of them. A risotto made with the selfsame rice from the selfsame Lombardy. Our trips were a lot more leisurely, though, and a lot less dangerous, tootling down the Po River in a motorized rubber raft belonging to our friend and culinary captain, Massimo Vitali. Off in the morning after a cup of cappuccino at the corner bar and home again in time for a glass of Barbera before bed.

I have only awe for the trek that Thomas Jefferson made, partly by seasickening boat, partly by spleen-jarring carriage, and finally, feet dangling to the ground, on the back of a mountain-climbing mule. Up one side of the Alps and down the other. Not to sit flushed and full of risotto in a sunny trattoria in a simple country village, but to smuggle the seeds, to grow the rice, to *then* make risotto. In perpetuity. *Che bravo.*

What passed through his mind as he went doggedly onward? I had to wonder. What thoughts fixed his sight on his goal? Was it, in fact, the lure of a creamy risotto that kept him going? By which I mean, was he on the trail of a memorable meal, many meals, as it happens, or were his motives purely patriotic? "I have ever considered the addition of an useful plant to the agriculture of a country," he wrote, "as an essential service rendered to it . . ." After all, the original purpose for his posting to France was to assist our ailing trade negotiator, Benjamin Franklin. Was Thomas Jefferson merely doing his job?

I couldn't quite believe that. Not that I doubted his sense of duty, not even for a second. From everything I'd read, I knew that his sense of civic responsibility was irreproachable, that he tore himself away from Monticello again and again to serve the republic he'd helped found. But I also knew that his interests were limitless and that he brought to each one the same enthusiasm that he brought to gardening. Architecture was his "delight." Music was "the favorite passion of my soul." He loved fine wine and good food. His dedication to science was renowned.

It was with great relief, therefore, that I went on to read about his side trips for sightseeing, and eating, to Turin, Genoa, Milan, and more. About his gratifying appreciation of "the abundance to be seen here." From the Charterhouse of Pavia to an icehouse in Rozzano, from frescoes to checkerboard marble floors to the theater. I was sorry he felt the wedding-cake cathedral in Milan to be "among the rarest instances of the misuse of money," but was glad we agreed on mascarpone. His discovery of this "rich and excellent kind of curd" brought back memories of my own exquisite first taste. Which then started me hoping he'd gotten to try it between layers of gorgonzola cheese. Or melting into steaming polenta. Washed down with a glass of Barolo.

Appetizing as this reverie was, it had a more interesting outcome still. I found myself wanting to, well, compare notes. With Thomas Jefferson. His marvel and delight were so similar to my own, several centuries later, that I wanted to find out what it was like when he visited Italy and to fill him in on the way it is now. Our relationship metamorphasized yet again. I began addressing him in the first person. No more third-person circumspection.

"If you were there in April," I would say, for example, "were the almond trees still in bloom? Were the tops of the hills lost in clouds of almond blossoms?"

A moment later I would add, "Speaking of almonds, did anyone offer you a glass of Amaretto? They make it right there in Saronno, you know, not twenty miles from where you were gathering rice."

I never expected answers to my questions. After all, I wasn't crazy. Nor did I ever consider them a conversation. Conversation implies more than one person talking and, as far as I could tell, mine were the only lips moving.

By the time I started talking to Mr. Jefferson, my winter recess was long since over. So long, in fact, that I'd already finished raising my seedlings and was in the garden planting them. My resumed occupation hadn't hampered my new activity, however. Quite the opposite, it seemed to thrive out in the open, under the dazzling June sky.

As the season advanced, the scope of my chat grew wider. I no longer limited myself to documented subjects, but talked about anything that struck me in the garden at large. "Isn't that a beauty?" I would say to him, picking a vivid red 'Sparkle' strawberry the size of Roger's paw.

"Do you think I should fertilize the asparagus in the fall or the early spring?" I would rub the hollow spot under my chin as I usually do whenever I'm undecided. "If I do it in the fall and it's a mild winter, it might leach past the roots by the time they need it in the spring," I fretted. "On the other hand, if I pile manure on them in late fall, it could also act as a mulch all winter."

By mid-July these types of comments had become so completely unconscious that when they started showing up in my garden notes, it was no surprise. They came in with the tomatoes. "*Jeffersonia diphylla* blooms on TJ's birthday, April 13th. First ripe tomato on my birthday, July 21st. 'Early Girl', not 'Simon'."

The next step was even less surprising. Inevitable, really, all things considered. The next step came on October 24th, a gray and miserable sort of day shortly after I'd put my garden to bed for the winter and was feeling bereft. Restless, I stuck a piece of paper in the typewriter and hammered out a letter. "Dear Mr. Jefferson," it began. I started out telling him about a map I'd just drawn, but wandered off on a dozen tangents before I got back to the point and wrapped it up. I signed off with a phrase I borrowed from him, a phrase whose eighteenth-century civility remains unmatched today.

If I felt a tad ridiculous when I started the letter, by the time I got to the signature, I felt on top of the world. There it was. I had my pen pal. And it was every bit as satisfying as I'd once imagined. What better way to chase post-frost depression than by writing about my garden. And about his. About how they tasted and smelled and what they meant. About gardens in general. About gardens in history. About the history of gardens. And their future.

It was great. Maybe it wasn't like being knees down in the dirt, but it was gardening on a new plane. I felt so shot full of vigor, actually, that a short time later, after a trip to Monticello, I sat down and did it again. Then again when the first seed catalog arrived. And again when I ordered. And again and again and again.

When spring came, and regular gardening began, I found it difficult to give up my new habit. For one thing, I had a narrative going, bringing Mr. Jefferson up to date on the gardening events of the past few hundred years, even as I brought him up to date on the current events in my garden. I didn't want to abandon him just when things started growing.

For another thing, though, I was enjoying myself. It was no longer a substitute for being knees down in the dirt, it was in addition to it. It was a new perspective on gardening, enlarged and enriched by thinking of it in terms of history. The letters kept coming through the spring and summer.

Just as I never considered my spoken comments a conversation, I never considered my growing collection of letters a correspondence, which, again, requires of the recipient the favor of a reply. Thomas Jefferson said it himself. "In matters of correspondence as well as of money, you must never be in debt." The last thing I wanted was to cast him into my debt.

Besides, *I* was the one replying here. *I* was the one responding to his volumes of letters and to the entries in his garden diaries spanning fifty-eight years. Certainly I assumed a few things about him, his attention, for starters, but I never presumed to put words in his mouth or thoughts in his head. God knows there are enough people doing that already.

Nor did I ever stray far from the garden path. Although Thomas Jefferson's interests and impact were staggeringly diverse, it wasn't difficult for me to resist taking detours. Like the Massachusetts Horticultural Society Library, sitting in splendid solitude above the honking and hurry of everyday life, I concerned myself solely with *affaires du jardin*.

My letters and comments continued all season, through the full cycle of the garden, from penciled plan to the doorstep of harvest. Neither conversation nor correspondence, they weren't a soliloquy either. Very decidedly, they were addressed to Mr. Jefferson. If he hadn't been at the other end of my thoughts, cultivating radicchio and tomatoes, journeying over the Alps in search of rice, fair skin tattered from the sun, very decidedly, those thoughts would have gone unsaid.

Okay. Maybe I am crazy. Maybe I'm hearing voices and writing to ghosts. But I still say that if this is a conceit, it isn't a caprice. It came about gradually, evolving naturally, and the first thing that every gardener learns is that Nature is a force you can't ignore.

Dear Mr. Jefferson

Today, in orchestrating one of the final acts in this year's garden, I also staged one of the first acts in next year's. Today, in order to plant the tulips, I made the map.

I do it every year, for if there's one thing I've learned about gardening, it's that those lush, bountiful beds of summer, bright and ambrosial, spilling like cornucopiae onto the grass walks around them, aren't achieved by inspired whim in the spring but by careful planning in the winter.

There are twenty-seven beds in my garden, maybe more, depending on how you count. Some of them are on the small side, holding only an eyeful of flowers, but others are big enough to yield a whole year's worth of onions. A few of them are planted with a perennial crop, like asparagus or strawberries or herbs, but most of them have vegetables that move from plot to plot every year, almost like musical chairs, except that nothing ever gets left out, as I am more apt to add a bed than to eliminate a plant.

With so many beds, though, I don't dare trust planning to musical chance or, worse yet, to my memory, because I surely don't want the potatoes to follow the eggplant or the tomatoes to come after the potatoes, and when the garden is freshly tilled in the spring, I can't honestly say which bare, brown rectangle held what last August.

Awhile ago, embarrassed to be responding to questions

about the size of my garden with "Oh, it's big. Very big," I measured it out. That isn't as simple a task as it sounds because the enclosed area isn't exactly geometric. In fact, it's shaped more like russet baker. This irregular configuration has less to do with the latest in design principles than with topography.

When Jimmy and I bought our property and cleared the house and garden sites, we were scrupulously careful to avoid cutting down trees. On an island whose thirty-two thousand acres are mostly heathland, scrub oak, and sand, the few hundred-odd acres of hardwood forest are precious, and each and every tree is revered.

I'm not fooling about that, either. We even have a trust fund for our trees, in a manner of speaking. It's an organization called The Nantucket Tree Fund and it's been raising money since 1982 to rescue trees in need. Granted, the neediest ones have been the one-hundred-and-fifty-year-old elms, which cast stately shadows across the cobblestones of Main Street, and which are dying, ineluctably, of Dutch elm disease. Still, it gives you an idea of the great regard we have for trees here, a regard I'm sure you can appreciate, as I know they were your horticultural passion until, under pressure of advancing age, you felt you'd better switch to flowers.

There are two trees on our property (we are lucky enough to live on the edge of one of those rare forests) that I hold in particularly high regard. One is a big tupelo growing by the side of the stream. About two feet up, its trunk forks, one half yawing out over the driveway. I find it picturesque. Idyllic. Delivery truck drivers have a different interpretation, cursing it roundly when their wheels come within inches of slithering into the stream as they swing wide around it. When Jimmy was a scalloper, bringing his boat home at the end of every season, he would have to fit the overleaning branch with a sling and hoist it up enough to let *Gale Winds* pass underneath. It's been threatened with amputation by chain saw, ax, and UPS assault, but in the latter case, the familiar brown box truck fared the worst, and in the former cases, I've stood fast.

The other tree of which I am especially fond is a venerable red maple of muscular build. Because of almost constant wind, laden with ocean salt, nothing on Nantucket grows very tall, but this red maple makes up for it in width. It's easily eight feet around and seventy feet across. In the summer, it's a cool, green retreat, its massive boughs nearly perpendicular to the spongy moss and wild strawberries below and broad enough to stretch out upon with a pair of binoculars to watch a red-tailed hawk making effortless loops above. In the winter, this maple is a magnificent sculpture, its heavy branches dipping and twisting, Medusa-like, one reaching almost to the garden fence more than forty feet away.

That branch is the reason there is no ninety-degree angle in the southeast corner of the garden. Other branches and other trees, less grand perhaps but no less esteemed, are the reasons that the garden is shaped like a potato, not like a blueprint, and thus is so difficult to measure.

Measure it I did, though, on that day. After a fashion. When tape measures failed, rolling themselves up or shimmying away from the starting mark, I abandoned them and strode off the dimensions, picking two pairs of opposite points pretty much at random. My balance being what it is, my strides weren't exactly even and my progress across the garden wasn't exactly straight. Nevertheless, I can now report that the garden is ninety feet by a hundred and seventy feet, give or take some strides. That's over fifteen thousand square feet! More than a third of an acre. I dwell on this only because I myself am amazed. As I've always said, it's big.

Certainly not as compared with the thousand-foot-long kitchen garden at Monticello, but then again, you had many more mouths to feed. Just to begin with, there was your daughter Martha and her husband, Thomas Mann Randolph, who managed your properties while you were away managing our burgeoning democracy. Then, of course, there were Anne Cary, Thomas Jefferson, Ellen Wayles, Cornelia, Virginia, Mary, James Madison, Benjamin Franklin, Meriwether Lewis, Septima Anne, and George Wyeth, all Randolphs, who came along in succession from 1791 to 1818, and all of whom, they say, you named.

Word has it that there was also an interminable procession of friends, relatives, and rubberneckers who would appear on your Palladian doorsteps with their families and staffs and who would not take their leave for days, weeks, or even months. Some were obviously more welcome than others, James Madison, for example, for whom a guest room as well as your seventh grandchild was named. From all reports, though, every visitor was graciously entertained, your hospitality being well known throughout the twenty-four states and one "federal town" that existed in your lifetime. Especially in Washington, D.C., in fact, where there's gossip to this day about the frequent dinners you gave while president, about your legendary wine cellar and excellent table.

Eating well, very well, appears to have been a priority of yours, and although historians, for reasons I've never comprehended, are usually far less fastidious about culinary details than they are about wars and inquisitions, a favorite Jeffersonian cuisine has emerged. It's a combination of Virginia country and fine French, always making allowances for your preference (nearly two centuries ahead of your time) for vegetables.

I wonder how many of your guests lived "temperately," as you once wrote that you did, "eating little animal food, and that . . . as a condiment for the vegetables. . . ." Whether as side dish or entrée, though, there were, undoubtedly, a lot of vegetables served at Monticello, making the two-acre terrace garden carved into the side of your mountain seem a completely reasonable size.

By the same token, I don't feel that my third of an acre, carefully draped over a rise and around trees, is an exaggerated size, even though there are only two of us at home, with an occasional weekend guest, and a few Christmas baskets to fill. Two of us, that is, if you don't take into account Roger and Homer, who most definitely are part of the household but who are indifferent to the temptations of a sun-warmed tomato or a plate of haricots verts and arugula, though Homer has been known to accept a proffered strawberry or to gnaw at a carrot the way he would on a bone. For purposes of vegetable consumption, however, neither they nor Jack and Olive, who are perfectly content with Science Diet supplemented by mice, voles, and, in Olive's case, moths, are enumerated.

Similarly, our chickens, currently thirteen Cinnamon Queens, all hens, aren't counted. Although *they* are vegetarians, with the dietary exception of grubs, bugs, and bacon, I've found them to be just as content with bolted lettuce and overblown cucumbers as with prime pickings. Weeds are also a favorite, and they'll fall upon a bushel of chickweed with the same relish I reserve for the first asparagus of spring. I must confess, too, that they don't really share the same niche in our hearts as do Roger and Homer, Jack and Olive. They are dear girls, and they lay enormous, orange-yolked eggs, but they are given to complaining, long doleful clucks, the way chickens so often are.

The ducks, however, are a different story, and although not in the dog and cat class, they have advanced in our affections to the point where they have names. Horace and Louise, buff runner ducks, begat Lily and Claudia. To her discredit, though, having laid the eggs, Louise completely lost interest, and it fell to a nameless hen, only too happy to fill in, to hatch them out. In infancy and ducklinghood, Lily and Claudia were convinced that the chicken was their mother, although they now recognize, and indeed prefer, their biological parents, traveling around the chicken yard with them, sitting when they sit, moving left when they move left, a perfectly synchronized duck ballet. The ducks are also vegetarians, and with no bacon exception, but they, alas, don't make the count either.

It wasn't always as large, this garden. The first year, it was just a single plot, an unremarkable tangle of zucchini, tomatoes, and resurgent brambles. The second year, I raked more assiduously after tilling and added some organizational paths. Pleased with the results, I grew grass in the paths the third year and laid out a series of beds, bisected by a twenty-foot-wide boulevard.

By the fourth year, another factor started figuring into this annual expansion, a factor both less tangible and less practically motivated. Somewhere between simply tidying up the tangle and standing back to admire what I'd done, I was overtaken, unbidden and unawares, by a sensation approaching passion.

It's difficult to define exactly. To call it a fascination creates an impression of disengagement, of peering through a microscope or over a museum case, hands clasped behind the back. Calling it an obsession goes too far in the opposite direction, besides failing to encompass the humor and enjoyment that are also a part of it. "Absorption" sounds like a sponge, "intrigue" like a court plot, and "addiction" too diseased. It's a state of mind every gardener has experienced since the first one dropped a seed in the dirt, watched in unadulterated delight as it sprouted and grew, then searched the neighborhood for new seeds to try.

I don't have to tell you about this state of mind, though. I don't have to explain the sensation that gripped me out there among the grass paths and vegetable beds. It was that same, ageless combination of curiosity and delight, as much as eleven grandchildren and countless visitors, that stretched your mountain terraces well beyond what was needed merely to feed your household. Just as it was responsible for swelling my garden from a radish-shaped bed to one the shape and relative size of a russet baker.

You once wrote, "I am curious to select only one or two of the *best* species or variety of every garden vegetable, and to reject all the others from the garden to avoid the dangers of mixture & degeneracy." Although the consequences of "mixture," or cross-pollination, were far more calamitous in the days before replacement seed was only a postage stamp away, I would still be willing to bet that in all your long years of gardening you never did come up with that definitive list.

Wasn't there always just one more variety that you had to try? A new one, perhaps, or one glowingly endorsed by a friend. Or maybe a variety that you'd planted before but that had been washed out by early rains, or baked by a drought that turned your red clay soil to brick, or shriveled by an unexpected frost, or eaten to the quick during a midnight raid by rabbits. Didn't you feel you really ought to try it again?

I'd be willing to take this bet because of two words. "Curious" and "best." Because they wave like semaphors above your otherwise reasoned prose. They are instantly identifiable to anyone who has ever been compelled to sow a seed for the suspense of seeing what would grow or who has ever embarked on the quest for the crispest carrot or the sweetest beet. Or the prettiest pansies to ring the beds. As every gardener eventually realizes, there is no way to satiate such curiosity or to decide upon the best. There is only the pleasurably incessant need to keep trying to do so.

Take peas, for example, reputedly your favorite vegetable. Did you ever find the perfect one? In the garden diaries you left behind, you first mention a variety by name in 1768. 'Charlton Hotspur'. Later that spring, you noted sowing 'Spanish Marotto'. Two terms as president, an ambassadorship to France, and various terms as governor of Virginia, secretary of state, and vice president (though not in that sequence) later, more than twenty varieties of *Pisum sativum* had been given a chance at Monticello, the most lastly named ones being 'Leadman's Dwarf', 'Leitch's', 'Marrowfats', 'Ravensworth', and 'Frame'.

It is a matter of stinging disappointment to me that I cannot find any of these varieties now. Which is not to say they aren't available somewhere or that I won't come across them someday, only that I can't lay my hands on them immediately or sow them in the pea bed this spring. I can't, in other words, relieve the maddening itch of curiosity that reading about them brought on.

"I have unluckily got out of the Ravensworth pea," you wrote to Richard Fitzhugh, "which I value so highly as to wish to recover it." How provocative that statement! What could this esteemed pea possibly taste like? And would it taste the same at my table as it did at Monticello a hundred and eighty years ago? Would the flavor of history sit with savory import on my tongue, even as the fat pods of 'Ravensworth' gave my garden a patina of times past?

There is a trend these days (we are a society rife with trends) of planting "heirloom" flowers and vegetables, some of which you cultivated, many others of which hadn't yet been bred or brought back from their homelands in remote regions of China or Peru or California. While I am not generally considered a trendy person, this is one that I, too, embrace. Not, I confess, for the earnest and wholly admirable purpose of preserving biodiversity, the battle cry of the movement. Rather, I plant heirlooms for the connection they make to other eras, for their tendrils that reach out and twine around history.

Just as the thought of a 'Ravensworth' pea growing in my garden transports me to your dining table, so does the 'Jacob's Cattle' bean, for instance, inch me closer to nineteenth-century New England. To wrestling with rocky fields. To sending daughters off to work in the woolen mills of Lawrence and Lowell. To smelling beans slowly baking in maple syrup and mustard on the back of the woodstove.

The same way that 'Clara Butt' tulips evoke images of my Victorian counterparts. I'll be imagining them next to me as I tuck bulbs into the earth tomorrow, their mutton-leg sleeves rolled up, kneeling amid yards of petticoats and skirts, to plant a brand-new variety, the first of its brand-new Darwin class. More than likely, I'll ruminate about what life was like for these women, who washed their clothes in a tub and couldn't vote. You may be interested to know we are fully enfranchised now. Some of us have even been voted *for*. And been elected or appointed to several of the same posts you once filled.

Having written five historical novels, three of them set only a few years after 'Clara Butt' made her debut in 1889, I find that this sort of rumination comes readily to me. I've spent untold hours on countless days wondering what was being eaten for breakfast a hundred years ago, what kind of soap sat by the sink, what songs were being sung, what was coming up in the garden.

I wasn't just being glib when I said I don't understand historians, why they go on at great length about battlefields and speeches but barely give a mention to the contents of the cupboard. Or the closet. Or the market. For me, history is in the details of daily life. It's knowing what my day would have been like if I had woken up on a morning in 1889, or in 1768, or on April 25, 1813, the day you wrote to Richard Fitzhugh, putting in a request for peas.

When I was young, I wanted more than anything to have been born at an earlier point in American history. If I could have had my first choice, I would have lived in the West, in a prairie schooner bound for the California goldfields, or in a raw and brawling frontier town. Now that I am older, and history is less varnished, I've come to the conclusion that I am quite grateful to be living in the twentieth century, and, at that, on the eve of the twenty-first. I've become attached to certain modern developments, like antibiotics and enfranchisement and indoor plumbing. Words don't describe how glorious a hot shower feels after planting potatoes on a spring day turned rainy and raw.

Still, there's part of me that's taken by the world that existed before anyone I now know was alive. Although I no longer want to be living in that world, I wouldn't mind being a tourist. I still long to know how a day in April 1813 would have unfolded. Paintings from the period suggest I would have been dressed in a high-waisted frock and a beplumed bonnet. A few hours spent at the Nantucket Atheneum turned up headlines about our war with Britain and Napoleon's war with everyone.

If I had a 'Ravensworth' pea to plant in my garden, however, or a 'Frame', or a 'Leadman's', or a 'Hotspur', I could experience some of what was going on at Monticello that spring. Firsthand. Not filtered through the grand overview of history. Not rendered unreal by a drumbeat of headlines and a numbing rattle of dates.

Even better would be a day several months later when I plucked a mature pea from its vine, shelled it, cooked it, and popped it into my mouth. In my kitchen in Wauwinet, on Nantucket Island, on the cusp of the millennium, I could taste the same flavor that the third president of the United States tasted, four years after his retirement, when he sat down at three o'clock, as he always did, to dine. Awesome.

So I have another explanation, or excuse, as the case may be, for the size of my garden. Not only is it a source of food, it's a means of communication, living picture postcards from other centuries, or from exotic destinations, or from dear friends. They're even shaped like postcards, my rectangular beds, except, of course, for the ones that are pie-wedged, or rounded, or otherwise irregularly contoured because of the trees.

Not all the postcards are from long ago and far away, mind you, nor are all the messages momentous. There's a mass of yellow daylilies from Jimmy's mother, for instance, that arrived without a name or a biography. Over time, they've come to be known as 'Nancy's' daylilies, or occasionally as 'Wilton Lemons', after the town in Connecticut where Jimmy grew up and because of their citrusy scent. The 'Ravensworth' pea probably came by its name in much the same fashion, borrowing it from Richard Fitzhugh's home, ten miles on the Monticello side of Washington. Maybe we have an heirloom in waiting.

There's nothing new about any of this. People have been re-creating gardens from other eras ever since other eras existed. They've also been handing along seeds and plants that take a name from the last place they've been. Had I ever gotten my wish and been that little girl in a wagon train headed west, I probably would have had, secreted in a small box or tied in a square of cotton, some seeds from "back east." A year or so later, next to a hardscrabble cabin on a California mining claim, *Lathyrus odoratus* 'Nantucket' might have bloomed.

That last part is pure fantasy, of course, as is all the other daydreaming about cowboys and gold. During the days of the Old West, and at every other moment up until 1905, no one even distantly related to me was on the North American continent, the offshore island of Nantucket included. My ancestors were still in Russia, where, being Jewish, they weren't allowed to own land or to farm. I come to gardening with only twentieth-century credentials.

Another highly commendable characteristic of gardens,

however, is that they aren't the Social Register. They don't scrutinize your pedigree before they'll issue you a trowel and a hoe. Born fresh every spring, they ask only that their current custodians weed them and feed them and pay attention to their peculiarities. Barring natural disasters, they'll grow like crazy, no questions asked.

It's a good thing, too, because there aren't any 'Nishni Novgorod' cabbages in my garden, passed down through grandparents and cousins. Even so, there is a sense of history and tradition, just as there is a sense of curiosity, and one of commitment. Not to mention the sense that the people who live here eat really well. It's all right there in the twenty-seven beds.

Fortunately, when we first started this garden, Jimmy had the foresight, or the mania, to clear the entire site suggested by the outline of the trees. Way back then, the area seemed ridiculously large rather than barely big enough. It seemed enormous, even taking into account our intention of turning the upper portion into an orchard, starting with four dwarf fruit trees we'd been given as a new-home gift. As beds begat beds, though, and as gardener's syndrome smote me, the wisdom of Jimmy's excess became evident. Expansion is easy when there's a well-defined space to expand into. Make that a well-defined and well-protected space.

Did I mention that there's a fence around the garden? Two actually. Every dozen or so feet, along the whole perimeter, there's a ten-foot cedar post sunk two feet in the ground. Strung along the fence posts is six-foot-high cattle wire. Not to keep in cattle but to keep out deer.

They are as much a part of the woods as the trees and the stream, only they don't stop at the forest's edge the way my favorite red maple does. I suppose I should feel flattered that with all the delicacies to be found in their domain, fiddleheads and *fraises des bois* and high and lowbush blueberries, the deer would find my choice of plants irresistible. Flattery isn't the feeling that floods my heart, however, when I see the sun rising on twigs where it set on peach blossoms the night before. A tall fence does wonders for our relationship.

To thwart the rabbits, which are nearly as abundant as tourists on this island, and who have made it their collective mission to eat every tulip and hyacinth I plant as soon as it lifts its head above ground in the spring, we have overlaid the deer fence with three-foot-high poultry wire and buried it under six inches of earth. The only way to breach this fortress is through either of the two gates, sitting next to each other and guarded by twin sassafras trees.

The gate on the right is nine feet wide, ranch style, with a diagonal support and chicken wire, in a wooden frame. We swing it open in the spring to drive in truckloads of manure, or in the summer and fall to drive out bushels of onions and potatoes.

The gate on the left is for daily access and is only as wide as a wheelbarrow. At first, in fact, it was a screen door we salvaged from the dump, which looked really funky and cool but came unglued after a season or two. It was replaced by a straightforward, cedar-board gate, seven feet high and arched at the top.

Although the description of this enclosure has a slightly industrial sound, it's not unattractive at all. The fencing itself has weathered with time, losing the dull galvanized glare it had when new. Actually, from any respectable distance, the mesh is invisible, offering a view of the garden unimpeded except by the cedar fence posts and gates, which give it, on the whole, a rather farmy air. Also with time, certain vines have clambered up the wire, a wild grape behind the asparagus, to name one, and perennial sweet pea toward the front. These, in addition to the ones I plant annually, like hyacinth bean vine and *Cobaea scandens* and morning glories.

It's handsome enough that I think you might admire it, or at least find it an exceedingly inoffensive solution to a gnawing problem. Granted, it doesn't present as formal an appearance as the three quarters of a mile of paling fence, ten feet high, you had built, the boards placed "so near as not to let even a young hare in." Then again, woven wire wasn't an option for you at Monticello, as it didn't come along until 1883. And became so hugely popular, by the way, that five hundred and fifty-two styles of it found their way to market before the National Bureau of Standards stepped in to restore some order.

The real beauty of this fence, however, lies in the garden it allows me to grow within it, a garden not munched and stunted by four-legged marauders, or confined to just food. After many tulipless Mays, spent demoralized and defeated by rabbits, I finally figured out that I can have spring-blooming bulbs after all. All I have to do is plant them behind the fence. As long as I dig them up again when they're finished flowering to make room for vegetables.

Even this chore isn't as onerous as it first seems, because its dividend is double the number of bulbs for next year. Provided I do it right, of course, which means cutting off the spent blossoms and allowing the foliage to ripen. Which means leaving the plants to bask in the sun until at least the middle of June. Which means putting them, in the first place, into a bed that won't be needed until late. Which is why I have to know, on October 24th, where I'm planting what next spring. Hence the map.

Not that having it on paper means that the garden is cast in stone. Nothing is final until it's planted. Even at that point, things can, in theory, be transplanted. Although I haven't tried it with anything annual. Yet.

Still, there is an exquisite sense of satisfaction that comes with this yearly task, a sense that goes beyond the undisputed pleasure of drawing twenty-seven postcard-shaped beds, then jotting brief messages in each one. "Cucumbers." "Melons." "Popcorn." "Zinnias." Just a quick salutation hinting at the tales to follow.

That, right there, is the joy of making the map. It's that hint, that unwritten promise. "More to come." "See you soon." Because what better way to cope with the grief that accompanies a hard frost, with the melancholy of afternoon nightfall and the desolation of bleak, gray dawn, what better way to ease the feeling of displacement when it's too cold and too pointless to be in the garden than by writing, and reading, messages from the garden to come?

How heartening. How reassuring. The garden is all but done this season, but there will be another season. I know there will be. Look. I've got a map to prove it.

Please accept the assurance
of my great esteem and respect,

L. Simon

Dear Mr. Jefferson

Don't I feel foolish! There I was, going on about my map as if, for all the world, I was the first gardener ever to put plans on paper. Of course you made maps. Scores of them. Maps of gardens that got planted. Maps of gardens that got replanted. Maps of gardens that you would have liked to have planted if you'd had the time. Or if you hadn't come up with a better map still.

Some of the maps you made were neat and precise, like your copiously annotated 1778 plan for the orchard, or like an early design for Monticello showing perfectly rectangular flower beds, overlooked by hexagonal temples. But the maps I can really appreciate are the simple affairs, like the loops and lines you drew on the back of a letter to your granddaughter Anne in 1807. With quick, easy strokes, you laid out, on your vast back lawn, a Roundabout Walk, banded by flower borders, because ". . . the limited number of our flower beds will too much restrain the variety of flowers in which we might wish to indulge. . . ."

I've been looking at all these maps, the past few days, here on your "little mountain," matching the early-nineteenth-century drawings with the late-twentieth-century gardens. The one is amazingly, admirably, eerily faithful to the other. Almost as if Wormley, your gardener, was hard at work, with Anne, and maybe her younger sister Ellen, reading your instructions out loud and unwrapping the parcels of roots and seeds and bulbs you collected from your widespread sources and forwarded to them from the White House.

The truth is, though, Anne got married at the tender age of seventeen, only a year after that letter, and long before the serpentine walk was completed. Ellen, smart, charming, gracious Ellen, was in less of a hurry, but when she finally married in 1825, more wisely and happily than Anne, she moved to Boston, a formidable twelve days' travel away.

As for Wormley, he pretty much dropped out of sight after you died, though there was some talk of his becoming a servant for one of your great-grandchildren, no mention of what position. For his sake, I hope it was in the stables, as his first love was horses, not gardens, despite his excellence in that department. I'd venture a guess that he cared more for Caractacus, your favorite mount, and for Diomede, Brimmer, Tecumseh, Wellington, and Eagle, your fine driving bays, than he did about the five hundred October peach stones you once consigned to his care.

You must be aware that Monticello itself more or less disappeared after your death. Not physically, of course. The mountain didn't crumble, nor even the house fall down in a heap, but the extraordinary character of the estate, the lively mix of gardens, gossip, family, music, books, ideas, and visits by past and future presidents, generals, explorers, and Virginia planters, ceased to exist. Monticello passed into other ownership, the family dispersed, crowds of souvenir hunters made off with precious plants, and cattle grazed on the lawn where you'd once welcomed Lafayette in a tearful embrace.

Not to put too fine a point on it, there were financial difficulties that made it impossible for Martha, or any of her children, to retain possession of your home. They were those same sticky money matters that hounded you all of your life. How unfair that after all you did for America, indeed for civilization, you had to worry so about making ends meet. Although I have to say that it was hardly the first time in the history of the world that creativity and accomplishment weren't rewarded in the wallet. But don't get me started on *that* subject.

Fortunately for all Americans, and for me in particular on this sunny autumn day, Monticello, after a rough patch, came into the hands of Uriah Phillips Levy, a Charlottesville merchant. Levy believed that the homes of great men needed to be preserved for posterity, which is exactly what he and his heir did, through war and strife, until Monticello was purchased, in 1923, by the Thomas Jefferson Memorial Foundation.

Devoted as Mr. Levy was to your memory, however, and dedicated as his nephew, Jefferson Monroe Levy, was to restoring your house, neither man's sense of history seems to have extended to your gardens. Already ravaged by the aforementioned memento-hungry hordes, and further brutalized by the knuckleheaded apothecary who owned your home briefly, and who cut down your carefully curated trees, replacing them with mulberries during a short-lived craze for silkworm farming, your grounds went through some tough times.

Not to worry, though, you made maps. Scores of them, as I think I've said. So many, in fact, that when the Garden Club of Virginia stepped forward, in 1939, to put the gardens back where they belonged, no one was really sure, at first, just *which* gardens, exactly, belonged.

Fiske Kimball, the restoration architect, had finally cobbled together a plan that was actually in the blueprint stage when Edwin Morris Betts came upon a more elaborate version of the map you'd sent to Anne. This one carried your memo "planted and sowed flower beds as above." Out went the blueprint and the Garden Club got to work.

Led by Hazelhurst Bolton Perkins, the committee drove their cars up the mountain one night and shone their headlights across the lawn. There, more than one hundred years after the last prickly poppy and mignonette perished, more than a century after the last Jefferson/Randolph took his or her ease on a setting stone, there, ever so faintly, was the depression left by the Roundabout Walk. Mrs. Perkins was in business.

I think it's a shame that this brilliant bit of nocturnal sleuthing gets only a passing line or two in books or, as I first overheard it, from the Monticello garden tour guides. Personally, I prefer to let my imagination linger over the event. I take great delight in imagining this procession wheeling up to the West Lawn, in picturing a troop of garden-club ladies, dressed in sturdy poplin skirts and sensible shoes, descending from their Packards and Pierce Arrows (I'll leave it up to someone else to update you on automobiles) and squinting across the emblazoned ground, alert to every dip and shadow. A round of applause, please.

When the time came to restore your orchard and, my favorite, your kitchen garden, the methods used weren't nearly as dashing, although the scientist and paleontologist in you might marvel at them more. In the orchard, soil borings helped determine which of the four hundred or so fruit trees grew where. On the next terrace up, it took two years of excavations to establish the location of walls and paths. The digs also uncovered the foundation of the idyllic garden pavilion that was the only one of the various temples, pagodas, ornamental bridges, and pseudoruins you periodically longed for that ever got built. And now rebuilt.

Naturalized tulips and persistent perennials have given significant clues in the course of this ongoing project. A new science, being pioneered down at Poplar Farm, your getaway estate, can pinpoint plants by their phytoliths, which are microscopic skeletons that remain, forever, in the soil. But let's face it. The real guides to re-creating your gardens were your maps. Without your maps clearly delineating flower borders and vegetable plats and berry squares, without your maps unequivocably labeling bushes and trees and varieties of peas, Monticello today would be just a hodgepodge of old plants.

Instead it is stunning, and just as you planned it. There are wide, open lawns and the narrow, focused borders, the Roundabout Walk, the long stretch of vegetables, the acres of orchard, and the eclectic grove, all giving onto vistas of the magnificent mountains and valleys of Albemarle County. Just as you planned it.

Of course, only you can confirm that, looking down from Heaven, or wherever your spirit resides. "Say nothing of my religion," you wrote to John Adams. "It is known to my god and myself alone." So I won't commit you to an afterlife, but I will tell you I can feel your presence here.

I'm not talking about ghosts, either, about phantoms in waistcoats and pantaloons. On the contrary, I'm very grateful that there is no one here in nineteenth-century costume, nor any demonstrations of candle making, bread baking, or weaving. Virtual history, in today's parlance.

How much more appropriate that there is French mallow and great blue lobelia, castor beans and cardoons, wild crab apples and catalpa, umbrella magnolia, hyacinth bean vines, double columbine, and sea kale. They are alive, growing as they did when you lived here, in the same compartments and plats that you assigned them, looking and tasting and smelling to my eyes, tongue, and nose as they did to yours. Not virtual but real.

This is history in its purest form. Not as a detached look backward, not as an event long over, not as an era distant and quaint, but as a continuation, as the past being part of the present. I can't think of many places this happens, besides in the garden. Thank goodness you made maps.

Please accept the assurance
of my great esteem and respect,

L. Simon

Dear Mr. Jefferson

The first seed catalog arrived with today's mail, a slight, quiet volume standing out by its sheer simplicity in a stack of garish holiday gift suggestions, cacophonous pleas for cash, and oversized, silver-foilized Christmas cards smacking more of smugness at having been gotten out early and gotten over with than of good will to all. The catalog, on the other hand, is of modest dimensions and its paper cover is charmingly decorated with a colored-in woodcut of tomatoes and salad greens. It's from The Cook's Garden, a name I find reassuring in someone selling seeds. There isn't always enough attention paid to the relationship between growing vegetables and eating them.

All this notwithstanding, I resisted the urge to cast my responsibilities to the wind, to brew a pot of Ty-Phoo tea, and to lose myself for hours in the pages of plant descriptions, cultural tips, and garden chitchat. Instead I set the catalog in a pile, now one deep, and promised myself that once it had been joined by a sufficient number of other catalogs, I would sit down and make my orders.

Well, all right. Maybe I *flicked* through it before setting it in its pile. Maybe a bean or two caught my eye. Okay, maybe an onion, too. It had an Italian name, you see. 'Giallo di Milano'. My willpower falters in the face of either Italian or onions.

The Italian part because during the years I lived in Italy, I learned to pay very close attention to the relationship between eating and everything else in life. Meals when I was growing up

46

in mid-century America were more about protein than pleasure. Flavor meant rare, medium, or well done, and the more interesting cuisines of our many immigrants remained in their kitchens alone. When I set sail for Europe in 1968, olive oil was exotic fare, but so immediate was my enlightenment that within days of taking up residence in Susan's apartment in Via Senato, I was sopping the stuff up with sturdy bread, bought daily at the *panetteria*, for breakfast.

Again, though, I don't have to tell you how delicious this was, or even to describe to you my innocent wonder at the man who drove his three-wheeled truck from Napoli every month to peddle labelless jugs of rich, green olive oil around Milanese neighborhoods the way the Good Humor man sold toasted almond crunch bars around the suburban streets of my childhood. Again, you had it figured out two centuries ahead of your time when you wrote, "Of all the gifts of heaven to man, [the olive tree] is next to the most precious, if it be not the most precious . . . because there is such an infinitude of vegetables which it renders a proper and comfortable nourishment."

I can't think of any more "proper and comfortable" aroma, taste, or sight than a skilletful of onions gently sautéeing in olive oil. Mouthwatering as this is, though, that wasn't what stopped my eye in the onion section of The Cook's Garden catalog. What stopped my eye, and my flicking thumb, was that 'Giallo di Milano' were seeds.

Every season there is always at least one something in the garden that surprises me, one something that wildly exceeds my expectations or bowls me over with its beauty. Last season there were two such things, the first of which was onions. Last season I planted some from seed.

For all of my gardening life, I have always planted onions

from sets, tiny bulbs that are, in essence, miniature onions. Although onion sets, sold by the garbage-canful in every hardware store and gardening center, are rarely called anything more intriguing than yellow, red, or white, I had never before considered the more tempting-sounding varieties available from seed.

You have to understand that I've gotten a lot of my gardening advice from Jimmy, who was living during those years when I was in Italy on forty acres in northern California with several dozen other people, being self-sufficient. It was a sixties sort of thing to do. In any event, while I was gathering experience with eating good vegetables, Jimmy was gathering experience growing them. The relationship between *us* has flourished, though perhaps not solely for this reason, and certainly despite his endorsement of onion sets.

To be fair, I should tell you that his stance on this issue has a solid, albeit outdated, foundation. Jimmy, and the myriad other onion growers who believe that sets produce bigger, better, more reliable crops, are harking back to onion culture as it was in your day, when seeds were sown directly in the ground and the results were spotty at best. Indisputably, sets were an improvement.

But in 1891 a Mr. T. Greiner published a treatise, *New Onion Culture*, in which he described, in glowing Victorian verbiage, his method of starting onion seeds in hotbeds, or indoor flats, in early March and transplanting them to the garden in May, "[f]or the production of a full home supply of the very finest and largest onions." I can vouch for the fact that his method works.

Last season, unable to pass by onions called 'Mambo', and

'Prince', and 'Walla Walla Sweet' in favor of sets labeled red and yellow, I succumbed. Telling myself, and Jimmy, that this was only an experiment, I sent in my order for a packet of 'Copra', "unsurpassed for storage." 'Copra' because the name reminded me of the winters I'd spent in the Seychelles islands. But that's a story for another time.

When they arrived, I planted the seeds according to the no-nonsense instructions in the Johnny's Selected Seeds catalog, making eleven shallow furrows in a plastic flat full of sterile soil and patiently placing the little black chips of seed four to the inch. Less than a week later, the flat was striped with tiny erup-tions, as if a battalion of minuscule moles marched beneath the surface. The next morning, the onions emerged, thread-thin green shoots, bent over double from the effort. They grew that way for a day or two, the fragile loops stretching up and up until they gained the strength, or the mechanical advantage, for the tip to pop free and wave triumphantly in the air. I was in love.

I pampered those onions shamelessly over the next eight weeks, cooing as I showered them with warm water or adjusted their lights. They responded to my ministrations with exuber-ant growth. So exuberant, in fact, that the day soon came to fol-low Johnny's penultimate instruction, to keep the tops trimmed to four inches tall.

Fearfully, almost flinching, I snipped a scintilla from one of those dear, green threads, by now the thickness of twenty-pound-test fishing line. The onion never noticed. Emboldened, I took a bigger snip, reducing the onion to its prescribed height. If anything, it looked relieved, standing up straighter, freed of its top-heavy excess.

More confidently, I started snipping the rest. The room

filled up with the odor of infant onions, mild, milder than chives. Somewhere before I reached the ninth row, I had it down pat, using a technique I'd picked up by watching Thom, my friend the hairdresser, cut my hair for the past twenty years. I slid a dozen or so onions between my pointer and middle fingers and clipped neatly along the palm edge. Mr. Greiner suggests using "common" sheep shears for this task, but I opted for sewing scissors, which, for one thing, I already owned.

By the time I was ready to follow Johnny's final instruction, to transplant the onions to the garden at four-inch intervals in rows one foot apart, those original fragile threads were positively vigorous, easily as big around as young string beans, and bristling with short, sturdy roots when I pulled them from the flat. Without a whimper and barely a wilt, they adjusted to their new residence and kept on going. In ninety-six feet, I didn't lose a one.

I guess I ought to mention here that I also planted one hundred and sixty-eight feet of sets. For safety's sake. This was only an experiment, don't forget. One, I might add, that caused me a few anxious moments when the rows of sets shot up past the rows of healthy, but noticeably smaller, 'Copra'. "Maybe you should side-dress them," Jimmy suggested, kindly. I didn't answer. I didn't concede, either.

My faith was not misplaced. Slower to start, 'Copra' were also in less of a rush to finish, continuing to thrive for nearly three weeks after the sets flopped over and gave up. The real moment of truth came at harvest time, though. When the first 'Copra' popped through the mulch big, round, and perfect, my heart leapt with joy. I was beside myself with pride. It's a feeling that's repeated every time I slice into one and its juice dribbles down the cutting board and its crisp, pungent odor rises up to sting my eyes. I find myself grinning idiotically through my tears.

Small wonder, then, that the onion section of The Cook's Garden catalog arrested my thumb and commandeered my attention. The era of sets is over in my garden and a whole world of choices replaces red, yellow, and white. There wasn't a great deal of description about 'Giallo di Milano', and half of what there was I chose to ignore: ". . . great Christmas gifts." But it doesn't really matter. For now, it's sufficient to know it's both Italian and seeds.

Of course, I hardly have to explain this to you, either. Way back in 1774, when Monticello was barely begun, you recorded planting "cipolle bianche di Tuckahoe." Even given the fact that Tuckahoe is in the next county over, and nowhere near Tuscany, "cipolle bianche" has a certain ring that "white onions" can't match.

I think, therefore, you can appreciate the powerful attraction 'Giallo di Milano' presented and thus the great restraint I exercised in setting the catalog aside. Perhaps I did make a notation on the cover first, but it was only a brief one. And in pencil. Then I *absolutely* put it down.

Please accept the assurance
of my great esteem and respect,

L. Simon

Nantucket
December 20th

Dear Mr. Jefferson

It occurred to me today that I got so carried away, last time, telling you about onions that I never even mentioned what the second surprise of last year's garden was. Here it is now. *Mirabilis longiflora.*

For a time, when I started gardening, I thought that calling plants by their botanical names, with that flat, Latin unwieldiness, was an affectation, a bit of horticultural snobbery. Now that I've moved along, and gotten the hang of it, I defend the practice as being eminently useful. If ever there was a perfect case in point, *Mirabilis* is it.

Bernard M'Mahon called it Marvel of Peru in his catalog, though its origin is more like Mexico than South America. In any event, by the end of the century, it was more commonly known as Four O'Clock, for its habit of blooming late in the afternoon. I have found Seven O'Clock to be more accurate, but that's quibbling.

When it's grown at all in gardens these days, it is pretty much as James Vick described it in his 1895 Floral Guide. "Grows two ft. high, bright foliage, fragrant flowers, and desirable colors. . . . Makes a nice summer hedge if set a foot apart." Packets of seed were 5¢. Although to my nose, the rather nice fragrance is evident only close up, the "desirable colors"—magenta, yellow, and white—of the trumpet-shaped flowers are vivid and noticeable from a distance. This, however, is *Mirabilis jalapa*, Jalapa being a town in the Tabasco state of Mexico, from whence, presumably, jalapeño peppers also come. But I'm not talking about them right now, either.

What I am talking about, what startled me last season with its ethereal beauty, is *Mirabilis longiflora*, seeds of which Bernard M'Mahon sent you in 1812 and the Garden Shop at Monticello sent to me in March. I don't know how many you received, but I got nine. Seven of them germinated.

After that point, I lost track of them. Not literally, of course, because if there's one thing at which I excel, it's making labels and lists, but in the spring rush, I no longer paid close attention to them. For one thing, I was coaxing along hundreds of other seedlings, but for another, *M. longiflora* wasn't looking a whole lot different from *M. jalapa*.

It continued to look not a whole lot different as it grew in its cell pack, and even when I transplanted it to an empty spot in the border. Maybe its foliage wasn't quite as bright. Maybe the heart-shaped leaves seemed larger and flatter. And yes, it wasn't standing up quite as straight or acting like a hedge. In fact, it could be said to be spilling. Since the empty spot where I'd stuck it was in the front of the border, however, and since the spilling was taking place over the edge of the railroad tie, I considered this difference fortuitous. That is, when I thought about it at all.

Then it bloomed. There it was when I walked past one evening, the first flower, illuminated by the twilight, new and fresh in the fast-fading day. A long, slim tube rose up from a pair of dusky leaves and flared into a snow-white, five-pointed star. From the center of the star, from its rose-tinted throat, came seven filaments, half the thickness of corn silk and colored the brilliant orchid of royal robes. Balanced on the tip of every fila-ment was a gleaming gold anther, each tiny dot as bright as the beacon from Sankaty Light in the gathering gloom.

I was spellbound. This was nothing like *M. jalapa* after all, a pretty enough flower but, by comparison, a trifle gaudy. This flower, this *Mirabilis longiflora*, was like something a fairy would conjure. It was like the clarion a fairy would sound to summon dragonflies and ladybugs and wood nymphs to a tea party on a lily pad.

Or perhaps it was like the trumpet an angel would lift to Heaven, an angel with rosy cheeks and holly wreaths, heralding Christmas. Maybe that's why it occurred to me today, maybe the pictures on the Christmas cards reminded me. *Mirabilis longiflora*. It was a Christmas present come early, an exquisite gift, a single flower, lustrous in the August evening.

> Wishing you a merry Christmas
> and peace on earth, I am,

> L. Simon

Dear Mr. Jefferson

Maybe calling it an epiphany is overly dramatic, but this went well beyond the realm of ordinary realization. One day, and not so very long ago, either, it just came to me that what my tangle of zucchini and brambles had evolved into was a kitchen garden. A *kitchen garden.*

That might seem obvious to you, or to anyone else from either of your centuries. After all, what else could such a collection of vegetables, flowers, and fruit trees be? Even given its potato-shaped perimeter, its occasional irregular bed, and its off-center paths, it almost exactly fits the description of kitchen garden as planted for centuries in Europe and imported, nearly intact, to the colonies. Only the contents of the garden changed with its transatlantic passage, expanded actually, as Indians introduced their new neighbors to corn, squash, pumpkins, sweet potatoes, and beans.

The design of the kitchen garden wasn't altered, though; the basic blueprint, so to speak, stayed the same. It was still a rectangle or a square, neatly quartered by paths and enclosed by a fence to keep the beasts at bay. Within the fence, which ranged in material from piled brush to brick, depending on the gardener's pocketbook, was a series of "digged" and "dunged" raised beds. Into those beds went seeds and plants, with a heavy emphasis on herbs, which served as salads, seasonings, and medicaments for everything from labor pains to lice. Somewhere inside, often espaliered against a brick wall if there was one, were as many fruit trees as the size of the plot permitted. Planted with strict adherence to moon phases and starlight, this was the typical kitchen garden when you first committed peas to earth.

Except for the beds, which aren't raised, and the sowing schedule, which is anything but astrological, it is also what my garden has become. All right, I don't have a *huge* selection of herbs, either, although I'm planting a few more each year for the bees, but the concept and the spirit are unchanged. My garden is still an enclosed area, subdivided into geometric beds, decorated around the edges with flowers, and given over to growing food. It is, unquestionably, a classic kitchen garden.

Why, then, I had to wonder, was this such a startling discovery? Partly, I suppose, because it just snuck up on me. I never meant, at the outset, to do what I've done. As I've told you before, my garden grew in gradual increments, and I guess I continued to think of it as a vegetable patch long after it had left its modest beginnings behind.

A larger part, I decided, has to do with the nomenclature itself. *Kitchen garden* simply isn't a term used much these days. At least it wasn't until quite recently, and now it's already in danger of being overused, which means it will next, inevitably, be distorted and then, ultimately, discarded in disdain. Be that as it may, some of the surprise I experienced was finding the phrase again and seeing what an unconscious fit it was.

Pleasant as these realizations were, however, they hardly qualify as epiphanous. What really swept me away was not the unpremeditated size of my garden, or even the delightful fact that it bore an honored name from the past. What really sent a bolt through my being was the realization that I was growing my own food. I don't mean a show-off summer salad or a bowlful of string beans. I mean food. Lots of it. A kitchenful.

Crates of potatoes and sweet potatoes and onions and squash are stacked up in the cellar. Jars of dried beans and popcorn and pickles line the pantry shelves. It's been a decade or more since I've bought a tin can of tomatoes. There's a freezer stuffed full of them. Along with green beans and petits pois and strawberries and sweet corn. We eat our surfeit of asparagus and eggplant in season, as well as chard and bell peppers and fennel and greens. I cut broccoli and brussels sprouts until Christmas and gorgeous bouquets of kale until spring. I pull carrots and leeks and parsnips and beets until it's time to replant the bed. There's always a head of garlic in the windowsill bowl and hot peppers and rosemary and sage. And not to forget Jimmy's honey or the eggs the chickens lay. Serious, sustaining amounts of food.

Again, this may seem perfectly ordinary to you and your contemporaries, even a shade meager for any postcolonial American who expected to eat. The difference, you see, and why it was such an eye-opener for me, is that most of us here in the twentieth century don't go to our gardens to get the ingredients for supper. We go to the supermarket instead. Better yet, we do takeout.

The United States, alas, is no longer an agrarian society. We're so far from it, in fact, that less than three percent of the population lives or works on a farm. The vision of America you described in your first Inaugural Address as a land rich and fertile enough for "our descendants to the thousandth and thousandth generation" has gone awry. It grieves me to tell you that hardly any of us has *seen* an amber wave of grain, let alone *grown* one, and more devastating still, more children than not have no idea that a potato is born in ground, not in a french fry machine at McDonald's. (Don't ask.) Odds are, they don't even know that french fries *are* potatoes.

This depressing state of affairs is due most immediately to a chain of events that began with those tin cans I mentioned, the ones that no longer darken my kitchen door. Strictly speaking, they weren't our invention, being the marriage of a French process of preserving food with an English creation of containers made from tin. Nor is the idea all that modern. Nicolas Appert, the Frenchman involved, came up with his concept of boiling sealed-up food in 1809, the same year you returned to Monticello, after two terms as president and a lifetime of public service, to begin a long, bucolic retirement, with your best gardens still ahead.

It was about thirty years later that the Englishman, Peter Durand, introduced his tin container, but really it was we Americans who made it all work. In a pitch-perfect example of our emerging national character, we started cramming everything edible into cans, faster, better, cheaper, and selling them to a public infatuated with anything new and convenient. They caught on like wildfire, especially after soldiers demonstrated how handy they were to carry into war. Did you know we had a doozy starting in 1861?

Frozen foods weren't nearly the sensation when they hit the market in 1929. Not that Clarence Birdseye's meal-sized boxes of creamed spinach weren't appealing. It's just that so damned much equipment was involved.

I don't mean only at the factory end, where miles of pipes

carried gases, dubbed Freon, on cycles of compression and expansion to create cold. No, the equipment shortage came after the frozen blocks of vegetables were produced. There had to be a way of getting them, rock hard, to market, a way for the market to keep them frozen until customers could buy them, and a way for the customers to keep them from melting until it was time to cook. I'm sure you can see the problem. Something was needed that was a little more compact than an ice house, like the one you had built in 1802 and stocked with "62 waggon loads" of ice in March of 1803.

Of course American can-do came up with solutions all around. There was never any doubt that it would, although this time the process was considerably hindered, first by a great depression and then by a world war. By the time it all got sorted out, another link in this peculiar food chain had been forged. The supermarket.

In the supermarket we were able to give full expression to another national trait. Our admiration of hugeness. Since the first supermarket opened its doors in 1937, these gargantuan stores have steadily increased in size, though not, it is my duty to tell you, in architectural charm. You could slide Monticello between the dairy cases and the dog food aisle of the average Stop & Shop.

Needless to say, as the interior space expanded, more products were invented to fill the added shelves. Again paying homage to our preference for new, fast, and easy, these inventions ran to "foods" like heart-shaped, rainbow-hued cereal and spray cans of cheese.

As for takeout . . . no, I'm not going to touch that one after all. Suffice it to say that Americans not only don't go to their garden for ingredients anymore, they've abandoned ingredients altogether. Today we want our meals ready-made. Cooking is considered a hobby. Small wonder, then, that kids don't know where french fries come from, or that peas have a natural package called a pod.

To be fair, this sad state is not the sole reason for the decline of kitchen gardens. In fact, it would be more accurate to say it is as much a consequence as it is a cause. Americans began to move, inexorably, away from rural areas to urban ones long enough ago that you were able to bear witness. The movement gained speed as the nineteenth century grew older, even though our vast continent was being thrown open for homesteading and settlement at the same time. Despite the aura of romance that made land rushes and pioneers the stuff of legend and pulp fiction, the fact is, cities were filling up far faster than the former Indian territories. Immigration and manufacturing were to blame.

As a man of the Enlightenment, indeed a pillar of the Philosophical Society that believed cultivating the earth was man's noblest calling, this news must be a bitter blow. "We have an immensity of land courting the industry of the husbandman," you wrote in your book *Notes on the State of Virginia*. It was your ideal, and that of your fellow Physiocrats, Benjamin Franklin among them, that dominance of this industry would define the New World. You had all seen the grim march of manufacturing across Europe and wanted no part of its "exterminating havoc" on this side of the ocean. Fresh air and farming paved the road to democracy.

Nice try, guys. Unfortunately, it wasn't to be. Manufacturing came, and so did the teeming cities that accompanied it.

Lawrence, Massachusetts, for one example, sprang up out of cow fields to support the new woolen mills flanking the Merrimack River. Population density was six hundred people, speaking forty-five separate languages, for every acre of dirt. And even if, by some sleight of hand, space for a garden could have been found, everyone in Lawrence over the age of nine was employed, twelve hours a day, in the mills. Physiocracy took a dive.

Dismal as this sounds, I don't mean to imply that kitchen gardens completely disappeared. Despite the overflowing cities, there were still plenty of people with land. What did happen, though, was that the classic kitchen-garden design, unchanged for generations, suddenly caught up with the times.

Before anyone knew it, raised beds were eliminated. Not just flattened, brought down to ground level, as it were. No, beds of all description were eliminated. Straight rows became the rage. "[A]n American garden for American farmers," trumpeted *American Garden Magazine*, preferring the look and practicality of a Kansas cornfield to that of an English estate.

Aiding and abetting the proponents of this new style was the invention, in the 1840s, of a curious device called the wheelhoe. Propelled by people power, it could zip down those straight rows in no time flat. "A boy of ten can keep the garden in perfect order," the *Arkansas Gazette* assured, offering a free wheelhoe to every new subscriber. A two-dollar model, however, not the deluxe Planet Jr., which came with cultivator, rake, plow, and seed drill attachments and cost, retail, $10.00, but could be found, by the shrewd shopper, for as little as nine.

Straight-row gardening wasn't without its casualties, as I'm sure you've already figured out. The first tradition to go was the profusion of herbs. Because when you're wheeling an arrow-straight furrow the length of your garden, all those perennial hyssops and tansies and elecampanes get in the way. Besides, by this point, in the upper reaches of the nineteenth century, there were patent medicines available to replace old-fashioned herbal cures. I'm not sure what could replace strawberries and asparagus, also perennial obstacles in the path of the plow, but I suppose that's where canned food stepped in.

If you think you are skeptical so far, listen to what came next. Next the luminaries of the day recommended ending our traditional dependence on nature to keep the garden pest-free and thriving, suggesting we adopt chemical means to do the job, instead. An influential voice in favor of this approach belonged to Liberty Hyde Bailey, Cornell professor and horticultural writer, but the name most often invoked in defense of chemicals was, believe it or not, Charles Darwin. His theories proved the superiority of man, went the argument, hence man-made arsenics of copper and lead, with alluring names like Paris Green and London Purple, were bound to be more efficient than beneficial insects for getting rid of the less welcome ones. Similarly, fertilizers scientifically concocted in laboratories had to be more nourishing than the haphazard meltdown of the old compost heap.

There was, of course, considerable resistance to these notions, mostly from the old-timers who believed, as you did, in the value of manure. "We will try this winter to cover our garden with a heavy coating of manure," you wrote to Martha in 1793. "When the earth is rich it bids defiance to droughts, yields in abundance, and of the best quality. I suspect that the insects which have harassed you have been encouraged by the feebleness of your plants. . . ."

Other behind-the-times gardeners felt that birds were the surefire remedy for holding those unwanted bugs at bay. Henry Ward Beecher was one of this school. To those who protested that birds did more harm than good, eating grain and pecking at ripe fruit, he rejoined, "The fruit is theirs as well as yours. They took care of it as much as you did. . . . They only come for wages."

Unfortunately, the reverend, and others like him, were out-shouted. By the end of the nineteenth century, the straight-row/chemical crowd held sway. They maintained their power well into the twentieth century, though they presided over an ever diminishing domain, because not only did the number of people with kitchen gardens shrink in size, the gardens themselves did, too.

Gone were the days when a book titled *How and What to Grow in a Kitchen Garden of One Acre* could find an audience, let alone a big one, as it did when it was published in 1888. Modern garden dimensions ran more to "plot" or, as my early one did, to "patch." And as I mentioned before, even the term *kitchen garden* fell into disuse. It seemed a bit of overkill to so describe the few tomato plants and head or two of lettuce stuck into a strip alongside the garage wall. Kitchen gardening moved, as cooking did, into the realm of hobby.

Again, don't get me wrong. There was always a hard core who kept the faith. There were even a few instances, down the course of this century, when the faithful saw their tiny ranks swell. One time was during that Great Depression I spoke about, and then there were those two World Wars.

One of the few bright outcomes of those terrible conflicts was the Victory Garden, a reincarnation of the Kitchen Garden of yore. Born of both patriotism and necessity during World War I, it enjoyed a great revival when canned goods were rationed and vegetables were scarce during World War II. Rallying support for the home and community garden in 1942, Secretary of Agriculture Charles Wickard urged, "Let's make it the three V's—Vegetables for Vitality for Victory."

As everyone pitched in for the war effort, rutabagas replaced rosebushes in suburban gardens, beets and carrots sprouted in formerly vacant city lots, and even kids enlisted in the School Children's Victory Garden Army. A whole library of literature was rushed into publication, because so far in the dust had we left our gardening roots that instructions such as "Watering must be done during dry periods" were imperative. If it wasn't precisely beating swords into plowshares, at least the weapons on this front were hoes and shovels, not guns.

What I can't understand is why, having once experienced the pleasure and satisfaction of gardening, people weren't permanently hooked. But, sad to relate, as soon as peace and prosperity returned, most of those proud Victory Gardens went down in defeat. In fact, only one time this century was a gardening boom, motivated by crisis, not immediately followed by a gardening bust when normal life resumed. That single instance was after the one-two punch of oil shortage and inflation in the 1970s. Not all the new gardens gained during that period of economic lumpiness went over to weeds when the Excessive Eighties rolled in.

By then, though, there were a few other factors involved. For one thing, Americans were developing an environmental conscience. The wake-up call had come in 1962 when a naturalist named Rachel Carson wrote a very scary book called *Silent Spring*. In it she let us know, in no uncertain terms, just how seriously we had trashed our continent with, get this, *chemical pesticides.* Indeed, she said, we had endangered the entire globe.

Out of the shock this bombshell created rose an earth-awareness movement in which gardening found a comfortable niche. Organic gardening, that is, which Jerome Rodale, its longtime and prolific promoter, defined as "a system whereby a fertile soil is maintained by applying Nature's own law of replenishing it. . . ." Hadn't you already said that? More eloquently?

Along those same lines, and at about the same time, another movement was afoot in America. This one could be called health awareness, I suppose, and its focal point was food. Not, I hasten to say, that we hadn't been eating all these years. Au contraire, our average, ample girth will attest to the fact that we'd all eaten more than enough. Don't forget about supermarkets. But now we were realizing that instead of those oversized steaks we'd equated with nutritional nirvana, we should have been chowing down on vegetables and grains.

Knowledge of vitamins, and of their importance, had been around since the turn of the century, and vegetarianism was . . . well, I don't have to tell *you* how long some people had been singing the praises of a vegetable diet. Dr. William Alcott, who opened the nation's first health food store in Boston in the 1830s, was a tireless advocate of eating only vegetables, fruits, and bread. He could wax positively poetic when writing about the rewards of this regime. I am loathe to report, therefore, that he and his fellow members of the American Vegetarian Society were regarded, when at all, as, uh . . . a little extreme.

Now, nearly at the end of the twentieth century, we are in the midst of yet another gardening resurgence. Although most of this one is about perennial borders and decorative beds, more and more of the new gardeners are taking up vegetables, too. For the most part, their reasons for doing so aren't dissimilar from those of the generations who preceded them. Homegrown vegetables cost less and are healthier to eat than the ones from the store. But the current gardening craze also owes its existence to a few other influences peculiar to the present. First and foremost among them is our discovery, at last, of the far-flung flavors of the world.

Finally, we have as a nation discovered the delights of Thai food and Greek, of Japanese and Indian, of Mexican, Chinese, Northern Italian, and Middle Eastern. Even the old stalwart, French cuisine, has been revisited. We have come to crave foods we'd never even heard of a few years ago, from the instantly ubiquitous pesto and salsa and salads of mesclun to the somewhat more particular pleasures of baba ghanouj and gnocchi and tortelli di zucca. Nor have we ignored our own regional specialties or seasonal offerings. Steamed fiddlehead ferns and filè gumbo have gone global, in a manner of speaking.

So it is that people who in the past would never have bothered to grow tomatoes for their BLT's or cabbage to make coleslaw are suddenly planting 'Principe Borghese' tomatoes to sun-dry and pak choi for their stir-fries. They're growing cilantro, and fennel, and cornichon cucumbers, and daikon, and jicama, and quinoa, and mâche. Purple broccoli are also coming up in these gardens, along with striped beets, and brown peppers, and eggplants that are lavender, or rose, or blushed, or white.

Which brings me, palate primed, to another aspect of this flavor revolution. Some gardeners, myself included, are not growing different vegetables so much as different varieties of familiar old favorites. Varieties, I might add, that have never graced a supermarket bin. Varieties bred for their irresistible taste, for their tantalizing aroma, for their sumptuous, savory, lip-smacking essence, rather than for their unblemished form or their shipping-proof skin.

Last summer, to illustrate, I grew seven varieties of potatoes, only one of which I have ever seen for sale commercially and all of which put store-bought spuds to shame. Same thing for the tomatoes (nine varieties), and lettuce (five), and shelling beans (six), and I think I've already told you, at some length, about the onions. When it came to sweet potatoes, however, I must admit that last season I restricted myself to one. My reason for this was simple. 'Porto Rico' is, hands down, bar none, the sweetest, moistest, most succulent tuber ever to cross my table. Had I grown any other variety, it would have been wasted.

But before I digress any further, and start giving you recipes or something, let me mention another singular factor of gardening's most recent rebirth. Baby boomers. Yes, I can well imagine you cringing. I do myself every time I hear the phrase. It's a silly sobriquet, especially considering it's attached to the most significant population impact our country has ever known. It's an entire generation, you see, an immense batch of people, all born in the affluent aftermath of World War II and all, at the moment, settling into middle age. It is also the generation of which I am a member.

By our sheer numbers, our every tantrum and trend has affected society, and the United States today is in no small measure a reflection of the growing pains we have never been shy about sharing. Presumably mature, at last, or at least worn out, we are now embracing the pleasures of, don't laugh, families, homes, and gardens. And following the pattern of every other stage we've gone through, we act as if we invented them. Certainly, we've given them our own spin.

This being the case, when an invitation arrived awhile ago to attend a symposium in Boston on The New Kitchen Garden, it's easy to understand why I accepted. To be honest, if my friend Ken hadn't mentioned that he was going, and if I hadn't had a dentist's appointment around the corner on exactly the same day and just at the moment the speakers were scheduled to break for lunch, I might not have been so quick to sign up. Boston is, after all, a two-and-a-half-hour ferry ride and a ninety-minute drive due north of Nantucket. But I did have a dentist's appointment, and it was at noon, so I went.

My first clue that this was not as serendipitous a decision as it initially seemed came when the leadoff speaker showed us a slide of Monticello and informed us that this was a "less successful" example of a kitchen garden because it wasn't enclosed. It had a "sense of fragility," he said. Less successful! Monticello! Fragile! Not only that, we also learned that grass paths aren't "desirable," and that if a bed isn't going to be raised, at least it should be bordered by a boxwood hedge.

Now, I am one of the last people on earth to ignore the aesthetics of any situation, let alone the visual appeal of a garden. Beauty is as important for the spirit as vitamins are for the body. But for me, the definition of beauty varies according to what it is I'm beholding, and when I'm beholding a kitchen garden, beauty is defined by vegetables.

To my eye, the beauty of a kitchen garden lies in its lush abundance and its promise of delicious meals. It lies in the lustrous sheen on a stand of Swiss chard and in the corkscrew brilliance of a ripe cayenne. It lies in rows of shell beans rattling in their October pods and in the sight, and maddening scent, of sun-blessed melons slipping effortlessly from their vines. It lies in the lovely lavender bloom of a bed of heirloom potatoes and in the robust bushes and shiny red fruits of nine varieties of tomatoes coming in.

"[N]o person has been more zealous to enrich the United States by the introduction of new and useful vegetables . . . ," Nicholas King wrote in 1806, entrusting to you the seeds he'd found wrapped up in an importation of Chinese tea. Somehow, I think, that zeal is more to the point of a kitchen garden than the fence that goes around it. Because if there's one thing that evolution has proved, it's that something to eat, some vegetable treat, has been the single constant element of a kitchen garden, whether of classic design or modern.

Which leads me, you may be relieved to hear, back to my original premise, which is my epiphany. Having brought you, and myself in the process, up to date on kitchen gardens, I guess I'd now have to say that the real surprise in mine isn't just the cellarful of food after all. I guess the real revelation, the real burst of enlightenment, is the realization that the garden I've created is part of a historical progression. It's part of an unbroken rhythm, an unstoppable cycle of seasons, part of a sequence of sowing and reaping that stretches from Roman times to Monticello to the cusp of a new millennium.

A kitchen garden is a document of society. It's a chronicle of the life and times in which it grows. I've always said that history is in the details of daily living, not in epic battles and stirring speeches, but when I made those grand pronouncements, I guess I never realized that with my potato-shaped kitchen garden, I was making history on my own. It took an epiphany.

Please accept the assurance
of my great esteem and respect,

L. Simon

Dear Mr. Jefferson

I've just returned from the post office, where I sent my seed orders on their way, mercifully ending three weeks of agony and indecision as I pored over catalogs, making selections for this year's garden. To be completely candid, this was not a miserable sort of agony or a distasteful type of indecision but rather the blissful torment of too many choices, all of them irresistible. Nevertheless, three weeks of this writhing is quite enough.

Granted, not all my choices were belabored. Some of my purchases have been exactly repeated so many times now that they almost come preprinted. I'm thinking particularly of the ⅛ ounce of 'Cut and Come Again' zinnias I order from Burpee, because I can't imagine a garden without an amplitude of zinnias, or the kitchen windowsill in summer without those crayon-clear flowers bunched in a bowl. And the packet of 'Jet Star' tomatoes I always buy and always from Harris. 'Jet Star' because they are unfailingly delicious, and Harris because that company developed them back in 1969 and thus deserves not only the credit for their innovation and industry, I feel, but also the profits. Park's 'Lindoro' carrots and Johnny's 'Triumph de Farcy' beans are somewhat more recent repeaters, but if they continue to please at their current, luscious level, I'm sure they'll qualify for this Hall of Fame, too.

There are a couple of more contenders: some melons, an

ageratum, a pea. Maybe two dozen or thirty packets in all. For the sake of round numbers, let's even call it fifty—out of one hundred and forty-five packets ordered. That means this year another ninety-five flowers and vegetables had to be deliberately, painstakingly chosen, one by one.

Some of the decisions were more elemental than others; only a straightforward yes or no was required. Should I grow salsify? for instance. Or *Phacelia* or *Verbascum* or mâche? Yes to the salsify and *Phacelia*, it turned out; a reluctant no to the *Verbascum* and mâche. It was at the next phase of decision making, however, that the real hand wringing began, especially where vegetables were concerned. At that stage, you see, having decided, in general, what I wanted to grow, I then had to pinpoint varieties.

'Snow Crown' cauliflower sounded awfully good, to show you what I mean. "Creamy white heads," The Cook's Garden described it. On the other hand, how could I pass up the "wonderful savor" of 'Montano', from the Shepherd's catalog, or the "excellent raw or cooked" 'Milkyway', offered by Parks? For that matter, just the name 'Cashmere' was mighty seductive.

I could go on from here, telling you how I dithered over disease resistance and days to maturity and hardiness zones. Before I've even recovered from the ordeal of the past three weeks, I could bring it all to life again, describing every tortured detail of it, seated cross-legged on the couch, pencils and pads and dozens of catalogs open all around me. It has occurred to me, however, that you may not know what I'm talking about.

Not just in the case of cauliflower, which from the first time you recorded sowing it in 1767, and for all the many times afterward, was never identified as anything other than

Cauliflower, let alone by a name as intriguing as 'White Sails' or 'Ravella'. Not unless you count your 1794 entry of "collyflower" or your occasional descriptive "Early." No, it's not the cauliflower I question, not the myriad, tantalizing varieties of this homely, white vegetable. Nor do I question the scores of tomatoes, nor the ambrosial assortment of onions. I don't question the head-spinning, taste-tempting selections of lettuce, or beets, or beans, or squash, potatoes, peppers, or peas. I don't question any of this because I feel certain the scientist in you could easily understand how so many new varieties came to overflow the catalog pages. What I question is the catalogs themselves.

I wonder about your awareness of the hundreds upon hundreds of catalogs in existence, of the thousands of pages beckoning the willing gardener with full-color photos or appealing illustrations, with untold numbers of inviting descriptions, with helpful snippets of cultural information. I wonder about your awareness of seed packets, and fruit trees, and rosebushes, and watering cans, all available by mail. Did you have any idea this was going on?

Again, I don't know how much you've been filled in on recent events, especially where gardening is concerned. There has been no end of people passing through the splendidly restored grounds of Monticello, starting with the people who restored it. You remember Mrs. Hazelhurst Perkins, I'm sure, and the Garden Club of Virginia. And I think I mentioned Professor Edwin Morris Betts, though only, as I recall it, in conjunction with the discovery of your map to the Roundabout Walk. What I neglected to add was that he also gathered all of your gardening correspondence and the fifty-eight years of your garden diaries into one stupendously annotated volume. Among other remarkable projects. Nor do I mean to exclude today's custodians of your gardening legacy, the contemporary keepers of the flame. They have done an extraordinary job of preserving your grounds and of adhering to the plans you made for them.

Conversely, that's what provokes my wonder. Monticello is not some footnote, you see. It's not some backwater, barely noted destination in a dog-earred guide. Monticello is a national treasure. And its past restorers and current preservers are the treasurers. So admirable is their work, so hugely, seriously, historically important, that it actually gives me pause. Are these guys too preoccupied? Do they have too much weight on their shoulders to just take their ease in the shade and engage in a leisurely chat? Or to update you on seed catalogs?

If they have clued you in, I hope you'll indulge me while I run through it all again, because if they haven't, this is something you wouldn't want to miss out on, I feel sure. Catalogs are the biggest thing to happen to American gardening since American gardeners started growing tomatoes.

Back before you started gardening, way back when we were just beginning, gardeners saved their own seeds or traded with their neighbors. Those with relatives left behind in Europe, or with a little extra cash, sent off to the Old World to diversify, or to renew, their stock. The colonies didn't stay small and feeble for long, of course, or even colonies, for that matter. But though we grew to twenty-four states in your lifetime, with ten million citizens and a distinctly entrepreneurial streak, this method of save/trade/barter/beseech remained, for the most part, the principal way seeds were dispersed throughout all of your gardening career.

A case in point is your message to Philip Mazzei in 1796. "I enclose . . . some seeds of the squash as you desired," you wrote. "Send me in return some seeds of the winter vetch. . . ."

Not that you weren't without certain commercial resources, even at that early date. If you didn't want to answer the proliferating newspaper ads (the first of which appeared in the *Boston Gazette* in 1719, offering "fresh garden seed of all sorts lately imported from London"), then you could have turned to the David Landreth Seed Company. Already twelve years old at the time of your letter to Philip Mazzei, the David Landreth Seed Company was the first of its kind in America.

Begun in 1784 by an English immigrant, who soon brought his brother into the fold, the company grew from being a modest truck farm that also produced seeds of "the first quality" to a firm that, by the mid-nineteenth century, had a worldwide reputation. American seed production hit the big time in 1847, when the Landreth Seed Company, as it was now called, bought three hundred and seventy-five acres in Bloomsdale, Pennsylvania, and started introducing its Bloomsdale seeds into commerce. Some of them are still around today. It wouldn't be spring for a lot of us, in fact, without a fat green row of 'Bloomsdale Longstanding' spinach breaching the cold, brown soil.

Although the family is no longer involved in it, the company is still in business and continues to bear the Landreth name. The new owners, proud of their acquired history, boast that you, along with George Washington, President Madison, and Joseph Bonaparte, were their customer. I'm not saying that isn't the case, mind you, at least as far as your trade was concerned. I will merely mention that, up until now, I haven't come across any evidence to corroborate it.

I have, on the other hand, found copious correspondence between you and John Bartrams, Jr. and Bernard M'Mahon, two other gentlemen of significance in postcolonial horticulture. Bartram, whose father, John Sr., and brother, William, were naturalists of great renown, made his own mark as a businessman, turning his famous family's Botanic Gardens into a large and prosperous nursery. In 1783 he issued a list of their wares, maybe not the very first such publication to appear on our shores but notable nonetheless for its great diversity and for its then unheard-of emphasis on native plants.

By the turn of the cenury, the nineteenth, that is, it was followed by an issuance of similar magnitude from Bernard M'Mahon. But while Bartram was devoted solely to nursery stock, M'Mahon had a broader range. Billing himself as a seedsman, he offered the seeds of hundreds of flowers, trees, vegetables, tender shrubs, and esculent roots. As well as a "large quantity of *Plants* and Cuttings of the most approved Vines. . . ."

M'Mahon called his circular A Catalogue, and so you referred to it yourself, but compared with what came later, this broadside was just a list. Just a single sheet of paper crammed full of eighteenth-century type. Just column after column of plant names and varieties, first in gardener's English, then in Linnaeus's Latin. No quantities. No prices. No descriptions. And certainly no helpful tips or garden gossip.

As the new century rolled forward, more and more of these seedsmen opened shop. Up in Boston, Joseph Breck launched his business in 1818, and what was to become Comstock, Ferre & Co. began across the line in Connecticut in 1820. I single these two out only because they are both going concerns today. But I'll skip over Thorburn and Bridgeman and all the others, since none of this is news. I don't have to tell you that these were the resources available when you were on your quest, say, for the Chili strawberry. I'm just taking a running start.

Before we get to the good part, though, I have to tell you about two other things that happened. The first was the railroad system and the second was a religious sect called Shakers. Again, this information may not be brand spanking new to you. There were probably abundant rumors about both. The English had been fooling around with steam-driven locomotives for years, finally getting their first train line fired up in 1825. Over here, the B & O line started running in 1830, and by the Civil War it had thirty thousand miles of track. And after the war, the railway system *really* expanded.

If you're wondering what this has to do with gardening catalogs, it's that stuff started moving around the country swiftly. Remember those twelve days it took your granddaughter Ellen to get from Monticello to Boston after her marriage to William Coolidge? With the advent of the railroad, she could make that same journey in a matter of hours. And of even more relevance to this discussion, so could a package or a letter. The U.S. Postal Service got its act together.

The Shaker influence is more direct and has nothing to do with the spiritual. What it has to do with is their incredibly simple innovation of packaging seeds in little envelopes they dubbed "papers." Being a self-sufficient and quasi-vegetarian group, garden seeds were of the utmost importance to the Shakers' survival. Not only did they plant them and improve their quality, they also sold them to the general public. In papers. Which William Comstock, of the aforementioned Comstock, Ferre & Co., jazzed up with decorative borders.

It was only a question of time before someone put all these elements together. In this case, fate decreed it should be an up-and-coming firm called B. K. Bliss & Sons, based, in those days, in Springfield, Massachusetts. About halfway along the nineteenth century, the seed house issued its history-making catalog. In it, they invited customers to mail in their orders with a payment, and to receive papers, now known as packets, of their chosen garden seeds by post. What an idea! It changed the face of gardening almost overnight.

The catalogs themselves had long since ceased to be the drab, single-page lists of the 1700s. Descriptions, almost too glowing, had been added, as well as varying degrees of horticultural instructions, all in the form of a book. So much had they grown, the Reverend Henry Ward Beecher was moved to complain, "We regard a very fat catalog as we do a very fat man—all the worse for its obesity." And that was *before* mail order started. Once everyone and his sons jumped on the bandwagon, seedsmen vied frantically for the gardener's attention with ever more magnificent catalogs.

In 1853 B. K. Bliss, once more on the cutting edge of the business it had pioneered, was the first to use color plates in its catalogs, making the flowers and vegetables it offered for sale seem intensely appealing. Next thing you knew, all the catalogs were illustrated.

Into the fray stepped James L. Vick, printer, editor, and self-taught gardener. When his horticultural passion lured him, in the 1850s, into the seed business, his former professions proved to be just the leg up he needed. Employing chromolithography, a new technique for printing color, he splashed the eye-catching paintings he'd commissioned across his catalogs' covers. On the pages inside, he projected an editorial voice that managed to sound warmly personal, while offering advice that was matter-of-fact and practical. Vick's Floral Guide, as he called his endeavor, was an instant success. Less than a decade after sending out his first volume, he had a quarter of a million customers, with more signing on every day.

He had also inspired endless imitators. The standard had been set. Multiple dozens of catalogs sprang up, each more alluring than the last. By the end of the century, in excess of eight hundred companies were in business, with overall sales increasing by more than fifteen hundred percent. And the catalogs! Oh, the catalogs. Chock-full of choices, they ran to unimaginable lengths. Forty, sixty, eighty pages, even a hundred or more was common.

Never in human history had so many flower and vegetable varieties been available for purchase. Peas, for instance. The D. Landreth Seed Company offered forty-two varieties of peas in 1895. D. M. Perry & Co. offered thirty-seven. They also offered thirty-one radishes, eleven kinds of celery, and sixteen different turnips.

When it came to flowers, Vick's Floral Guide showed again why it was a champion. The 1894 catalog listed twenty-six varieties of pansies for sale and, hold onto your hat, *ninety-five* kinds of sweet peas. Granted, the sweet pea was the most popular flower of the period, but ninety-five varieties?

This staggering selection was matched in tone by the engravings on every page. Gorgeous, tantalizing illustrations of caboose-sized cabbages and cucumber canoes leaped out at the browsing reader. Never mind that these drawings bore only a passing resemblance to the vegetables they depicted. Whatever they were, they looked delicious and were, apparently, impossible to resist. Sales continued to soar.

There's someone else you should know about, while we're on the subject of gargantuan success. His name was Washington Atlee Burpee, and he made it even bigger than James L. Vick. So big, in fact, that when Vick's heirs put the Floral Guide up for sale in 1920, the Burpee firm bought it and folded it, with barely a bulge, into its business, already the largest of its kind in the world. But that's jumping ahead a bit, ahead of the "High Class Land and Water Fowls" and ahead of the Scotch collie puppies.

Burpee's first catalog, launched in 1875, when he was seventeen years old, was a mere sixteen pages long and devoted solely to those above-mentioned birds. Livestock was added the following year, in partnership with a fellow Philadelphian. Seeds were actually an afterthought, offered only when the hogs they had for sale displayed an unanticipated preference for a particular variety of corn. And *only* that variety. It didn't take Burpee long to realize that the corn was a better seller than the hogs. In 1878 he shed his partners for good and put out a catalog on his own.

Yes, the time was ripe for his triumph. Yes, the huge middle class spawned by, sorry to tell you this, America's industrialization was a market waiting to happen. But Burpee, more than anyone else in the business, knew how to strike when the iron was hottest. I'm not saying he didn't have a good product. He did. The best. And he worked hard and inventively to make it even better. Where W. Atlee stood head and shoulders above his competitors, though, was in an area that we in the twentieth century call Promotion. Mr. Burpee was a master at offering incentives for people to grow his seeds.

He ran contests and competitions, awarding cash prizes for the biggest and brightest yields. Anything to keep his customers' attention. He also kept them coming back by offering an array of items they needed around the farm and garden. In addition to the standard lawn mowers and pesticides, he returned to his roots and offered livestock. Pigs, sheep, and fertilized chicken eggs, as well as the one that touches my heart: rough-coated Scotch collie puppies. Beautiful, brilliant, and incredibly sweet, they were the perfect farm family dog. Besides, it thrills me to speculate that Roger could be the descendant of a Burpee puppy, sent through the U.S. Mail.

Not one to neglect education, Mr. Burpee also published books. Certainly he wasn't the first to come up with this idea. Bernard M'Mahon, in fact, preceded him by almost a century. M'Mahon's *American Gardener's Calendar* went through eleven best-selling editions before being eclipsed by works from such seedsmen as Peter Henderson, Thomas Bridgeman, Robert Buist, and Joseph Breck, never forgetting, of course, James L. Vick. But while these gentlemen published their own well-considered, and weighty, Manuals, Burpee favored what he called booklets.

Nor was he the author, and this is where he broke new ground. He was the first to make sure that books got written, and published, on all the diverse subjects that informed the gardening public. Books on sweet peas, and poultry, and injurious insects, as well as a whole string of treatises on growing various vegetables for profit. My old mentor, T. Greiner, contributed the one on onions, avowing that "There is Big Money in Onions: $500, and even more, per acre, if you know how to get it out."

As a premium for large seed orders ($3.00 and above), a book called *How to Cook Vegetables*, written by the Principal of the Philadelphia Cooking School, would be sent along for the asking. "Broiled or baked blackbirds may be served with the salad course," Mrs. Rorer instructed.

All in all, it was a glorious era. With W. Atlee Burpee leading the charge, seed catalogs grew as fat and lush as the caboose-sized cabbages that illustrated them. The apex of this Golden Age was probably reached in 1901, when Burpee's Silver Anniversary catalog came in at an astonishing two hundred and twenty pages. After that, things calmed down.

Following their lavish burst of creation, and after American gardeners were firmly hooked, the seed companies started analyzing costs and weeding out their low-selling items. Then a World War came along, and wars are always hard on domestic business. Especially when paper is scarce and when a lot of your suppliers are overseas, in the battlefields of Europe. A whole raft of companies disappeared, though catalogs themselves persisted, and progressed.

Shortly after the war, the first photographs turned up on catalog pages, and by the 1930s, they were the standard illustrations. You probably aren't familiar with photography. It's a technology that came along after your time, but without going into a detailed explanation, let me just say that through the use of lights, mirrors, and silver salts, you come up with an exact image of that at which you are aiming. Pretty slick. Except that even the most flattering photograph of the most perfect flower or exemplary vegetable couldn't then, and can't now, match the sheer voluptuous excess of the old Victorian engravings. An element of reality crept into the catalogs, and reality is almost always sobering.

Twentieth-century catalogs swelled or shrank with war or peace. Their emphasis on flowers or vegetables shifted with the prevailing period. Across the board, though, the dizzying number of varieties sharply diminished, as indeed did the number of offerings in general. It was not, as you may remember me telling you, an adventurous time for gardening, or for food and fine dining, either. The national trend was toward a single American culture, a homogenized blend of all our ethnic identities. As long as it came out Anglo-Saxon in the end. There was no radicchio in these catalogs.

If you ask me, we have been, for a dozen or more years, in the throes of a Renaissance. If it can't quite be thought of as a Second Golden Age, then surely it can be called a New Generation of catalogs. This time around, though, it's not about knockout illustrations in bulging editions. This time it's about well-honed and highly sophisticated simplicity.

Instead of behemoth catalogs carrying everything in gardening existence, this time around there are small, tidy catalogs that concentrate, really concentrate, on a particular specialty. There are catalogs for just primroses, for instance, or just everlastings, or perennials. Catalogs for hot peppers, or giant watermelons, or onions, or potatoes. And didn't I already tell you about Totally Tomatoes? There are also catalogs that are region specific, like catalogs for the prairie, or the Pacific Northwest, or, one of my favorites, Southern Exposure Seed Exchange, which comes out of your own Virginia.

There are catalogs of only heirloom flowers, like Select Seeds, or Perennial Pleasures, which actually has its flowers indexed according to their century of introduction. There are catalogs of only open-pollinated seeds, catalogs of hybrids, catalogs of Asian vegetables, or Italian, or Native American. There are catalogs for trees, or for wildflowers, or for herbs. Catalogs of only fragrant plants, only alpine plants, only conifers. There's even a company that's so focused, it offers only *one* kind of seed, for 'Dr. Martin' pole beans. And I mustn't forget to mention the Thomas Jefferson Center for Historic Plants, which sells only seeds from plants grown at Tufton, one of your farms. With an addendum for seeds of other eighteenth- and nineteenth-century plants that could, in theory, have enhanced your gardens, though you left no records to prove it.

I'm not saying that there are *only* specialty catalogs today, that in order to plant a kitchen garden you have to hop from supplier to supplier. That's the way I used to grocery shop when I lived in Italy, back when the whole world was different. In those days, I went from the *panetteria* to the *latteria* to the *salumeria* to the *fruttivendolo*, gathering together the ingredients we needed to make dinner. It's a habit I've never entirely given up, even though, when catalog shopping, I can't stop on the corner for *un caffè* before returning home with my purchases, carefully wrapped up in paper and tied neatly with string.

I'm trying a new specialist this year, one called Tomato Growers Supply Company. They sell tomato seeds, as you've probably guessed. It's not listed first, but they do have 'Abraham Lincoln'. Two of him, actually. Original and Regular. I couldn't find 'Jeff Davis', although I did come across a

'President'. The biggest surprise, though, a surprise of jaw-dropping proportions, was the discovery of a tomato called 'Jefferson Giant'. They say it's an heirloom but give no indication of how it got its name, claiming only that the heart-shaped pink fruits are exceptionally sweet and that the vines are vigorous growers. I'm assuming, however—I'm not even considering otherwise—that its name is in honor of you, a tribute to your legacy. So much for my earlier indignation.

But I was trying to tell you about the general stores of the seed world, not the single-item shops, although I could interject here that Tomato Growers Supply Company has, besides three hundred and twelve varieties of tomatoes, one hundred and twenty-one peppers. Still, that's hardly what it takes to get a kitchen garden started. For that, there's a catalog like Johnny's. Johnny's Selected Seeds of Albion, Maine, is an excellent example of a catalog that offers the whole spectrum of seeds for the home gardener and does it in New Generation style.

By that I mean that Rob Johnston—a.k.a. Johnny, I guess—encourages organic methods of gardening (though he doesn't insist). He also searches out and promotes healthy vegetables from all over the world and, not incidentally, breeds many of his own. Although he does have the distressing habit of giving them cold, clinical numbers rather than taste-teasing names.

One thing Johnny doesn't do, to my everlasting gratitude, is strew recipes for cooking the vegetables among his descriptions of the varieties. This, I'm afraid, is an increasingly common practice. Johnny may note, briefly and informatively, that pak choi is ideal for stir-frying, for instance, or that the tomatillo is an integral part of Mexican cuisine, but he refrains, entirely, from instructing us to mash the potatoes with garlic or to toss the mesclun with hazelnut croutons and raspberry vinaigrette.

I know it seems like an anomaly, after all my posturing about vegetables and good eating, but I have to tell you, quite frankly, I don't think recipes belong in catalogs that sell seeds. That's what cookbooks are for. Susan, who has just written a luscious one, called *The Nantucket Table*, managed to go from Carrot Crostini to Gingery-Lime Blueberry Pie without ever once slipping horticultural advice in amongst the list of ingredients. Johnny's shows a similar restraint.

This might be a good time to mention that a lot of gardeners not only aren't consulting catalogs for recipes, they aren't looking at the seeds, either. Renaissance or no, the majority of seed packets sold in America today pass over the counters at garden centers, supermarkets, and hardware stores and not through the channels of the United States Postal Service. Today's crop of gardeners, stretched thin with kids and careers, doesn't have time to fret over catalogs or to wait for their seed choices to arrive by mail. Very often they buy and sow on the same sunny Saturday afternoon, quickly, before the impulse is lost. Or something else comes up.

Also, and this is even more critical, these busy gardeners buy fewer seeds in the raw, from any source, and more already started, pop-in-the-ground, the-garden-is-done plants. A huge slice of today's seed sales, therefore, is to the nurseryman, who, not surprisingly, is less interested in growing unusual or heirloom varieties than in growing those that are fast, fuss-free, and readily marketable. Naturally enough, this narrows the field for the seedsman, no pun intended. I think you can see where this is leading. The seedsman stops sowing the slow-selling seeds, and the next thing you know, they've gone out of existence. Diversity doomsday.

I am doing my level best to staunch this steady drain, ordering from nineteen different catalogs, out of the eighty-five or so that find their way to my mailbox, and shunning the ready-to-plant market. In fact, I consider it a point of honor to start all my flowers and vegetables from seed myself. With only three exceptions, I can more easily do without a plant than I can bring myself to buy someone else's seedlings.

Geraniums, though, which I could and should, but don't, start from cuttings every January, I buy bursting with buds from Bartlett's Ocean View Farm, across the island. I have, actually, started them from seed a few times, but they took too long to reach any significant size, and they never did catch up to the ones from Bartlett's, which only get more robust as the summer advances. Besides, I'm very fond of an ivy geranium called 'Harvard', which has a simple, single flower, the same rich plum as its namesake's color. If I get to Bartlett's before Memorial Day, I can usually snare a couple.

Of course, the geranium I really want is the one you had in Washington at the end of your presidency, the one Mrs. Samuel Harrison Smith pleaded with you to leave for her when you retired to Monticello. The one that would be "attended with the assiduity of affection and watered with tears of regret" at your absence, "the most venerated of human beings!" But since this geranium was not further identified, other than "neglected" when you turned it over to Mrs. Smith, I'll have to content myself with imagining it and making do with modern hybrids.

This, however, has nothing to do with exceptions numbers

two and three to my seed-starting rule, which aren't even flowers, let alone geraniums, but are potatoes and sweet potatoes. And which, when you come right down to it, aren't true exceptions, either. I mean, I could, in theory, grow both of them from seed, but that's a hair too obsessive, even for me. Potatoes grow with splendid success from other potatoes, cut into healthy chunks, eyes just beginning to bug out, and a sweet potato will make a whole new plant, including the tubers, when one of its leafy green shoots is stuck in the ground.

Although I have yet to coax into creation any of these shoots, known as slips, I do, every spring, cut up some of my own chunks. I cut them from potatoes I have stored in the refrigerator downstairs, insurance potatoes, stashed away after the last harvest comes in. A few pounds each of the two or three most essential varieties, the varieties without which life, and dinner, would be unspeakably dull. 'Bison', 'Sierra', and 'German Butterball' are the current trio.

Not that these are the only potatoes I plant every year. Not even close. There are always several less vital varieties, a couple that get completely consumed before they can make it as far as the refrigerator, and, of course, one or two new ones, just to try out. But these potatoes I order from Ronniger's. Wait till I tell you about this catalog. It's potato nirvana.

On a mountain bench in northeastern Idaho, in soil that's sixty inches deep, the Ronniger family grows seed potatoes. More potatoes than you can imagine. Red ones, blue ones, fingerlings, bakers. Potatoes for mashing, potatoes for roasting, potatoes for making into salad with fresh peas and chives. Potatoes that will keep all year long, or potatoes that should be eaten as soon as they're dug. Potatoes from Scotland, from

Sweden, from South America, from Canada. They even have an heirloom potato from a neighbor down the road. The Ronnigers grow a serious selection of potatoes.

Then they issue a catalog. On its newspapery pages, nestled among dark snapshots and glowing testimonials, are descriptions of the potatoes, written with such sincerity, such simple elegance, they seem like a letter from a country cousin, or maybe even like a story. The same can be said for the cultural advice that follows, advice as beguiling as it is good. I go back and read it several times a year, sometimes for the information, sometimes for pleasure.

By contrast, the catalog for Fred's Plant Farm, every bit the place to buy sweet potatoes that Ronniger's is to buy spuds, is but a single sheet of paper that also doubles as the order blank. There are no winning descriptions here, just little boxes to check for variety, quantity, and delivery date, along with an admonishment to add extra for shipping to "FAR AWAY PLACES," a category in which Massachusetts, evidently, is included. It's not much of a come-on, but, boy, those 'Porto Rico' sweet potatoes are good.

Now that I think about it, I could divide all nineteen catalogs along the same lines. Some of them I order from because I've been won over by their distinctive personalities or disarming voices, by their earth-kindly practices or their horticultural passions. Then there are catalogs—usually catalogs that on the face of it are impersonal or commercial, catalogs I collectively call tabloids for their large, glossy formats and full-color photos—that I order from because they deliver the goods.

Under this latter heading come catalogs like Harris and Stokes, Burpee and Park, catalogs that, by the by, have all been around for more than a century each. Harris's offerings, to be truthful, aren't awfully fascinating, but I am a fan of the founder, Joseph Harris, and they do have a nice mix of 'Springtime' pansies. I scrape together a few other choices, classics like 'Heavenly Blue' morning glories and 'Boy 'o Boy' marigolds, but probably, if it weren't for my loyalty to their 'Jet Star' tomatoes, I would pass Harris by and distribute these few purchases elsewhere.

Stokes is another one I'm tempted to drop, even though, quite the opposite of Harris, their selection is staggering. Especially in the vegetable department, my favorite area to shop. My quibble with them, however, is in their descriptions, which are conscientious enough but almost entirely devoid of the adjectives I'm seeking. Adjectives like "flavorful" and "delicious." Yes, of course, disease resistance is an admirable quality, but when it comes to vegetables, taste is my first priority. Still, it's hard to ignore all those choices.

Which brings me to Burpee and Park, the first two companies I ordered from when I started gardening, lo these many years. I don't know why it is, but despite their big pages and flashy photos, I've always thought of Park as modest and self-effacing. Maybe it's just by comparison with brash Burpee, although I'm more inclined to believe it's because of the respectful attention they pay to every plant on their list, never dropping old favorites or pruning back their extensive collection of hard-to-find flowers, no matter that these seeds may not be best-sellers.

Burpee, on the other hand, is right on top of every trend. If it's hot, Burpee's got it. If it's not, it's gone. I sometimes feel as though I'm in a new-car showroom when I'm browsing through the Burpee catalog. Everything is new and state of the art. Even the old standbys, and the few fashionable heirlooms, seem to be, by association, lacking in patina.

But it's easy to pick on Burpee because they are still the biggest target. Still, after all these years, the biggest mail-order seed house on the planet. And to be fair, despite all of the gloss and all of the drumroll, Burpee is also responsible for many, many flower and vegetable introductions, some of them important, some of them wonderful. 'Iceberg' lettuce, for example. W. Atlee brought it out in 1894, and though I neither eat it nor grow it, it's my duty to report that it is, otherwise, ubiquitous.

At the other end of the scale are two Burpee melons, 'Sweet 'n Early' and 'Ambrosia'. Probably unknown to the population at large, they are next to hallowed by anyone who has tasted the luscious, juice-dribbling fruits that come out of the garden. I shudder to think of Jimmy's reaction if, by some calamitous error, I failed to order these two cantaloupes, especially the former. It is his delight, a ritual almost as treasured as tending his bees, not only to breakfast on a melon just plucked from the late-summer, sun-mellowed garden but also to load a crate or two of them onto his truck and take them to work with him on the wharf. There he dispenses them like so many favors, a feudal king tossing gold coins to the grateful peasants.

But enough about the top dogs. I want to tell you about the ones that are nipping at their heels. The companies that don't develop seeds so much as collect them from many eclectic and far-flung sources. Yes, I'm talking about those new catalogs again. Though I qualify "new" as dating from the 1970s, coinciding with the beginning, in earnest, of the Earth Movement and with the first glimmerings of light on the gastronomic front.

Pinetree Garden Seeds fits perfectly into this category.

Begun in 1979 on the ingenious premise that since most gardeners never use half the seeds in the packets they order, there was the need for someone to offer small amounts of seeds at much smaller prices. Gardeners loved the idea. It was a way to try a new variety without investing a fortune. The one problem came when we ran the gamut of Pinetree's list, also small and, at the time, only so-so interesting. This is not a static company, though. The owner, Dick Meiner, started expanding, hand over fist. He brought in vegetable seeds from all over the globe, including an intriguing selection of hot peppers, privately collected. You could almost sense how much fun he was having.

As for me, my initial curiosity order of a couple of packets has taken off in recent years, to the point where my selections now overflow the page. Like Ronniger's, Pinetree has won me over from its prominent position in the distinctive personality/disarming voice camp. Because apart from the hot peppers and 'Matt's Wild Cherry' tomato, the flowers and the vegetables Pinetree offers, while many and unusual, are hardly unique. I could find these seeds elsewhere, if I really made the effort, but Dick Meiner's descriptions, with their miniature histories and conversational opinions, project a fascination that's utterly contagious. Of course, those small prices I mentioned earlier are a big draw, too.

Is that nineteen, yet? If not, it's probably close. The rest are small orders, anyway, like from Territorial Seed Company, a perfectly nice firm, but targeted at the Pacific Northwest. Out of my zone. Of course, Southern Exposure Seed Exchange is even farther out of my zone, but I so dearly love this catalog and its original offerings, I'll scour its pages until I find something that will grow in Nantucket. 'Fowler' bush beans, for one, are out of this world. And Southern Exposure Seed Exchange is my alternate source for 'Tennis Ball' lettuce, a tight, buttery variety that you often noted sowing, sometimes failing, at Monticello.

R. H. Shumway's is bizarre, like a Victorian catalog gone mad, but if I have the patience to page through it, I can usually find a gem. This year's is a popcorn called 'Dynamite Yellow'. The cost of the postage is more than the price of the packet, but I have a weakness for popcorn and Shumway, I've discovered, is the only mail-order company that carries this South American variety.

I could go on, if you like. Don't forget I get eighty-five catalogs, though a bunch of them are just for irises and daylilies and a bunch more just for roses. There are also another two-hundred-odd strictly seed catalogs I could send for, and although that seems like a lot, it's considerably fewer than the eight-hundred-odd that were around at the beginning of the century.

But that's got to be enough. I'm sure, by now, you've gotten the picture. I'm sure you can see how seed catalogs have shaped the course of gardening history in America. And how, having shaped it, they are now vital to America's gardening future. Gardeners no longer have the habit, as they did in your day, of saving their own seeds or trading with friends. Seed catalogs, then, especially the new ones, with their carefully curated lists, are the key to keeping alive a diversity of vegetables with deep flavor and flowers that have both fragrance and beauty.

As I've said, the new seed catalogs seem up to the task. The next step, though, is for the public to support them, to fill in the order blank and send in the check. It's too terrifying to contemplate the future if we don't. Those three hundred and twelve varieties of tomatoes might get reduced to a handful.

I'm proud to say that, personally, I'm doing my duty. I rose to the challenge and ordered one hundred and forty-five pack-ets, many of them heirlooms, from nineteen seed houses. It was three weeks of agony, but I loved every minute.

Please accept the assurance
of my great esteem and respect,

L. Simon

Dear Mr. Jefferson

Something I overheard at Monticello in October has been gnawing at me for the last four months. One of the garden guides, leading a group of visitors past the fish pond, turned to the tourists in her wake and remarked, "We say that Thomas Jefferson was a gardener, but we know he didn't actually do any of the work on the grounds himself." I was startled by the statement, and by the suggestion it left hanging. I've been brooding over the definition of a gardener ever since.

Is a gardener anyone who "likes or is skilled at working in a garden," as the dictionary says? And "working in a garden"— does that mean turning over the beds in the spring, harvesting the crops in the fall, and doing all the planting, pruning, weeding, and watering in between? Yourself? Does having help with these tasks disqualify you?

"When I go into my garden with a spade, and dig a bed," wrote Ralph Waldo Emerson, "I feel such an exhilaration and health that I discover that I have been defrauding myself all this time in letting others do for me what I should have done with my own hands." In fact, history does not remember him as a gardener but as a philosopher, a poet, and a proponent of Transcendentalism. Nantucket history remembers him as a nineteenth-century luminary who spoke on several occasions in the Great Hall of the Atheneum. As did Henry David Thoreau, now revered as a naturalist, who served, for a stretch, as one of those "others" who defrauded Emerson by doing his gardening. But I think I sense myself going off on a tangent. I was talking about having help.

For all the first-person possessives I apply to *my* garden, I have to confess that I don't do it all *my*self, with all due respect to Emerson's assertions of "exhilaration and health." First to help me with the garden, as with almost everything in life, is Jimmy. In April and early May, he's in charge of hauling in truckloads of manure and of rototilling the beds, a modern technique of turning over the soil involving machinery and noise. In the summer, he moves sprinklers and yards upon yards of hoses; in the winter, he ventures out on frozen afternoons to pull parsnips and carrots from underneath their straw mulch. Then there are the potato trenches and suckering the tomatoes, picking the melons and grading the onions. The list goes on and on.

In the old days, back, way back, before he had beehives, back when the garden had just evolved from a patch of zucchini and brambles, Jimmy and I used to spend every Sunday in the garden together, puttering around, doing whatever was necessary. Around teatime, Hilda, my mother, would drive up in her blue leviathan of a Pontiac, to come sit on an overturned milk crate while we sprawled in the grass, all of us eating ice cream sandwiches. Roger, there was only Roger then, would wiggle down next to me, tail swishing, soliciting kisses and pats. It was a very pleasant way to spend a Sunday, though I'll have to admit we did not make great inroads against the chickweed. The garden produced vegetables, but by the Fourth of July, it looked, in a word, awful.

That's when Dede entered the picture. When she hap-

pened to mention, one summer afternoon, that she was thinking about starting a gardening business the following spring, I
signed her up on the spot. She became half of Growing
Enterprises, the half that drives the truck and wields the tools.
The other half of the business is Hilary.

Hilary's mother was a golden retriever named Jolly, her
father just a stranger passing through on vacation. Hilary herself is a ninety-pound-plus brunette with hair that is enviably
wavy, beetle brows, and the merest hint of a beard. Lest you
think I am anthropomorphizing her role in the firm, I assure
you she is a tireless exterminator of predators, the four-legged
ones that can ruin a garden. Many a vole has rued ever finding
the sweet potato bed or the tulips, and Hilary's diligence in
routing out the rabbit who lived behind the cold frame was
nothing short of heroic. She barked at it, week after week, year
after year, her resolution never faltering, until it finally surren-
dered, deaf and defeated.

Fortunately, the improvements Dede wrought were more
immediate and more visible. The garden shaped up, looking
handsome from planting time till frost. Pleased and encouraged, I started expanding, adding five little beds, then three big
ones, then the two shaped like pie wedges. I experimented with
new varieties, indeed with new species, then moved on to the
landscaping, where I changed and rearranged most of those
plantings. Through it all, Dede humored me and offered endless helpful hints.

"You know, you can buy this stuff in cans at the supermarket," she let drop as we spent hours one morning digging a
deep trench for a new row of asparagus crowns. "Save you a lot
of trouble." Actually, Dede dug the trench. I stood at the foot

of it, ready with directions for refilling it with layers of peat moss, garden loam, and manure, playing the straight man to her quips. Oh yes. I also made lunch.

A lot of the other advice Dede gave me was more serious and more valuable. After all, she had worked, for years, on the farm down the road and had a degree from Stockbridge, the Agricultural School at the University of Massachusetts. Hold on. I should probably give you a quick update on Ag schools, considering your plea to establish "[i]n every College and University, a professorship in agriculture . . ."

"Young men, closing their academical education with this, as the crown to all other sciences . . . ," you argued in 1803, "would return to the farms of their fathers, their own, or those of others and replenish and invigorate a calling. . . ." I'm not sure when universities started offering agricultural courses, but the first institution devoted solely to that purpose, the Michigan State College of Agriculture, opened its doors forty-seven years after you wrote those words, Liberty Hyde Bailey being one of its early graduates. Now there are Ag schools all over the country.

Sad to say, however, the era of Growing Enterprises is over, at least in my garden. Hilary is still willing, but Dede has trumped her floriculture degree with one in early childhood education. Yup. She's going to teach school. Lucky kids. Unlucky me.

More than likely, my search for someone to replace her has sharpened the debate about what a gardener is and whether you lose that designation if someone else digs the trenches for the asparagus and potatoes. Not everyone, of course, weighs the answer so carefully. For Helena Rutherford Ely, whose assertive voice enlivened garden literature at the beginning of this century, there wasn't even a question. In her book *The Practical Flower Garden*, she wrote, ". . . [W]hat could be more heavenly for a woman gardener than to be able to grow all these flowers and plants, and . . . to have all the men she needed—really good and efficient men—to cultivate them. . . ." Clearly, Mrs. Ely had her priorities in order.

The conclusion I've come to, after four months of mulling, is that it's the tour guide, not me, who needs to rethink this issue. A gardener should be anyone who loves plants enough to create a garden, whether that means tending a few geraniums on a city windowsill or coming up with a plan to hew a thousand feet of vegetable beds out of the side of a mountain. Can't this please be one thing in our society that doesn't have a code of admissions and bylaws to follow?

"No occupation is so delightful to me as the culture of the earth," you wrote to Charles Willson Peale, "and no culture comparable to that of the garden." Considering that passion, and the results at Monticello, I can't comprehend how even a hint of doubt can be allowed to hang in the air. You were a gardener if ever there was one. What's more, those gardens were yours then, and they are still yours almost two centuries later, no matter whose hands actually operated the shovel.

The wonder isn't that you may never have stuffed a 'Marcus Aurelius' tulip bulb in the ground but that you took the time to order it from Bernard M'Mahon, to design a bed for it, and to make sure that it did get stuffed and in the spot where you wanted it, what with drafting the Declaration of Independence, serving as minister to France, secretary of state, vice president, and president of the United States. Twice. The wonder is that you found the time to imagine its perfect tulip bloom, to be persuaded to have it planted by its promise of spring.

One of the most appealing portraits of a gardener I've ever read was the introduction to *Onward and Upward in the Garden*, a collection of the exquisitely enjoyable writings of Katherine S. White. The introduction, however, was written by E. B. White, her husband, who described his late wife as a gardener of strong opinions and clear vision, a gardener who went among her roses dressed in tweed suits and Ferragamo shoes.

For all the enthusiasm and interest she brought to her gardens, though, "[s]he did little of the physical work of gardening herself; in youth she lacked the time, in age she lacked the strength. . . . But she masterminded everything . . . and we always ended up with a vegetable garden that loaded our freezer and nourished our bodies, and with flower borders that filled the eye and the spirit." I rest my case.

Please accept the assurance
of my great esteem and respect,

L. Simon

Dear Mr. Jefferson

I don't know how the idea of putting a screen door on the guest room came to me, but one day it was just there. The idea, that is. The screen door took a little longer, although idea and installation actually occurred in the same season, which, Heaven knows, is some sort of record. The door was hung today, and I am thoroughly pleased, impressed by my clever solution way out of proportion to the problem it solved.

It's a twofold problem, I should tell you, in my own defense, the first part being the cats, and the woodstove being the second. We heat our house with the latter, and have done so forever. Jack and Olive are relatively recent additions, having moved in a year ago, last November, after Jimmy finally wore me down. He was tired of waging war, single-handedly, against the rats who lived under the chicken house. It was time to call in reinforcements, he felt.

But I'd never had cats, you see, I've always had dogs, so I put up resistance, saying that cats were aloof and unaffectionate, that they were given to clawing the furniture and jumping up on the counters. Never, Jimmy denied, shocked at the very suggestion, remembering, somewhat selectively I'm sure, the perfect behavior of Tony the Cat and Thurman Munson from his childhood. The compromise we finally brokered went something like this: Yes, we would get a cat, but we'd better make it two, because the first one was going to live outside in the shed, so the second one would keep the first one from getting lonely.

This barn-cat scheme lasted about as long as it took to sign the papers at the MSPCA, adopting Jack, already two years old and a big, gray, pussycat bruiser, and Olive, a little bitty calico kitten with one eye that was permanently skewed. They came home and took up residence in the guest room, the door firmly closed, while Roger and Homer sulked on the other side of it, digesting this insult.

This, however, was not the problem to which I was referring, even though it did involve the cats and the guest room and the door to it, too. But notice the past tense here. This *was* a problem. It's not anymore. By Christmastime, everyone was on speaking terms, and Jack and Olive, having abandoned the guest room, were making themselves comfortable wherever fancy took them, to the chairs, to the couches, to the beds when Jimmy wasn't looking, or, in the case of Olive at this very minute, draped, head down, across my lap. Her purr is bigger than she is.

The problem in question, therefore, has to do with the secondary use of the guest room. Although I suppose it would be more accurate to call it the primary use, transitional dormitory for cats coming in third behind number two, accommodation of guests. First and foremost, though, for three months every spring, the guest room gets transformed into a nursery. For plants, that is, not babies. Well, baby plants, to be precise.

We lift up the bed and stand it against the wall, then lay a sheet of plywood on two sawhorses set in the middle of the room. At either end, and over the top of the eight-foot span, rises a double frame, a crude arbor, an unlovely four-poster canopy. Instead of vines, though, or organdy curtains, from this frame are suspended seven industrial grow lights on S hooks and chains. Let's see. Grow lights. Electricity. Uh oh. Out of my zone. Let me just say that grow lights are simulated sun.

And plugged in, as they are, to automatic timers, our simulated sun shines for sixteen real hours of simulated day.

The whole idea makes me a little uneasy, but the seedlings don't seem to object. Quite the opposite, they love it. Lined up in green plastic trays, twenty-two inches by eleven, cushioned on pillows of fine, fluffy soil, and showered, when thirsty, with gently warm water, these emerging plants are, with very few exceptions, delighted with their simulated spring. Oh yes, this is where the screen door comes in.

In order to keep the nursery warm enough for the seeds to germinate and the seedlings to grow, the door has to stay open, allowing the heat from the woodstove in the living room to waft upstairs and enter. But in order to keep Jack and Olive from mistaking the green plastic trays for their litter box and the seedlings for salad, the door to their former headquarters has to stay closed. I think you'd agree that a screen in this situation, barring cats but not heat, is a stroke of brilliance. Or, on second thought, considering the architectural elegance of Monticello and the University of Virginia, maybe you wouldn't. It works for me, though.

Self-congratulations aside, what's really worth talking about is what goes on behind the screen door for those three months when the weather outside the windows can still be less than inviting. Especially March. That's when I pass some of the most agreeable hours of the gardening year. Don't misunderstand me. Nothing beats the pleasure of being outside, real sun baking into my bones, the smell of damp, spring earth clearing winter out of my nose. But starting seeds is an act of such divine magic, of such supreme sorcery, that it has never yet failed to leave me astonished and glad-hearted.

It's a process that hasn't changed much since your day, or

even since time began. You drop a seed in the dirt, water it, and wait for it to sprout. That's kind of magical, don't you think? I mean, here's a seed, a tiny fleck of matter, smaller, in some cases, than the period that will eventually end this sentence. But inside its insignificant little carcass are the makings of a five-foot-tall delphinium, say, with flowers so twinkling blue they'll make you suck in your breath. What's more amazing still is that when you commit this delphinium seed to earth, it will always come up a delphinium, an identical copy of the delphinium that came before it.

What also hasn't changed is the feeling of hope. The sense of sublime expectation when the garden, and all its plants, exist in the imagination only. There are no weeds here, no aphids, no drought. For this brief time every spring, the garden looks, smells, and tastes the way the catalogs promised.

Nor for this interlude is there any cold rain or blisters. No mosquitoes, no sore muscles, no dirt-stained, sandpaper hands. These mornings and afternoons in the bright light and cosseting warmth of the nursery are like a lullaby, a mesmerizing miracle, they follow a cozy routine. Pick up a packet, snip off the top, lay the seeds inside down on their pillows of soil. Check the list to see how many plants I want to have in the end, then make the section of seedbed bigger or smaller accordingly. The trays are divided with wooden tongue depressors that I trade with Ken, a pharmacist, for cherry tomato, eggplant, and bell pepper seedlings. Cut into four pieces, once each way, they also serve to name the seeds in each separate bed.

In a few days, or a week, or two weeks, sometimes, a tiny green bulge breaks the surface of the soil. The next day two leaves stick straight out from a spindly stem. By and by, another pair of leaves appear to keep the first two company. Oh sure, all

babies are cute and adorable, but is there anything cuter than a baby verbena?

No, some things don't change at all. Not for eons, anyway. Baby plants are still, as they were when you grew them, the result of seeds, soil, and water. Even the seeds, I'm sure, look exactly as they did, some being just specks, others being admirably striking. Didn't your *Scabiosa* seeds, for instance, look like little lamp shades of pleated beige linen? Weren't your bachelor's button seeds like tiny whisk brooms just the right size for one of Gulliver's Lilliputian captors? And how about marigolds? Do you think it's really possible to tell just by looking that inside the seed of a marigold, with its black handle and pale straw fringe, resides a modern 'Queen Sophia' rather than one of the marigolds you ordered from Bernard M'Mahon in 1807?

When you come right down to it, the only thing that's changed is the manner in which we gardeners, over the centuries, have assisted Mother Nature in doing her job. Take those grow lights, as a good example, the simulated sun. Or the neat rows of identical green plastic trays, or even the fluffy pillows of soil that go in them. Some trays come predivided into green plastic drills, but I prefer the open ones that I divide myself, with tongue depressors, into miniature fields.

All this is different from the seed-starting methods that predominated up until early this century. Until then, most seeds were started outdoors in nursery beds, set off in a corner of the garden, or in cold frames, or, for an extra boost, in hotbeds, so named because the surface of the soil was heated to toasty by an underground pit of dung, decomposing and steaming. "The best manure for hot beds," Joseph Harris advised, in 1878, "is horse or sheep-dung that has been used as bedding for pigs."

Enamored as I am of connections to history, I think I'll stick to my guest room-cum-nursery. Without even addressing the issue of where, on Nantucket, to find manure that's been slept upon by hogs, there are a number of other advantages to my arrangement that are hard to overlook. For one, seedlings stand a much better chance for survival on their cushions of soil, which, it turns out, isn't soil at all but a sterilized mixture of ground-up peat moss and perlite with some vermiculite thrown in. No overwintering diseases lurking in these beds, poised and ready to attack tender, new roots. No doubts. No variables. Just an even, pampered environment in which seeds can germinate and grow. Besides, I like making a morning visit to the nursery in my nightgown and slippers, something I'd be reluctant to do with a hotbed in the middle of March.

Another historical option I've rejected, one I could more conceivably pursue, at that, is the suggestion you offered Mme. de Tessé in an 1805 letter accompanying, among other seeds, those of "*Juniperus virginica*." "[h]e crammed them down the throats of his poultry confined in the hen-yard and then sowed their dung, which has been completely effectual," you wrote, describing a propagation method employed by someone you knew. Even if I wanted some *Juniperus virginica*, which I don't, I'm not sure I could get the girls to consent to this chore.

In a similar vein, I mean the vein of seed-sowing advice, not of chickens or junipers, I should tell you about seed packets, specifically about the cultural directions that are usually on the back of the envelope. I say usually, because sometimes they are on the front side or, most annoying of all, occasionally they are missing. But when they are there, they are enormously helpful, eliminating a lot of the goofs that come from relying on memory. This probably wasn't a problem for you with your legendary mind, but I have to admit that my memory gets murky.

That's why it's nice to have, right there in hand, answers to the questions that inevitably arise. Yes, I know that baby plants are the result of seeds, soil, and water, but it's the particular combination of these components that I forget from year to year. Do the seeds want to be covered with soil in order to germinate, like tomatoes and asters, or exposed to light, like ageratum and snapdragons? Do they want to be chilled, like cleome, or soaked overnight, like parsley, or do they want to be sown in their own pots, like fennel and lavatera? See what I mean?

I'll tell you who wins, hands down, in the packet-directions department. Nobody comes even close to Harris for good, clear, pertinent information, and lots of it. Everything from light requirements to soil temperatures to how far ahead of time the seeds should be started. Arranged partly in chart form and partly as data, it finishes with specific planting instructions and is printed, bless their hearts, in plain, bold, large enough type. What a pity I can't find more things in their catalog to tempt me, and an even greater pity that most of their seeds come treated with chemical fungicides.

Coming up on Harris's heels is Seeds of Change, a company that, far from using chemicals of any kind on its seeds, grows all of them organically. Fairly new on the scene, Seeds of Change has recently undergone some changes itself. It is now much more accessible, and its seed packets are excellent.

I should explain that there's something else I do with my seed packets every spring. I line them up, according to sowing times, in a long, narrow drawer. I don't know how this drawer found me, or what piece of furniture it came from, but it is just the right size to hold one hundred and forty-five seed packets plus some cardboard dividers.

Assuming Memorial Day weekend to be zero, I work backwards, weekend by weekend, until I get to ten, which is when I start heliotrope and verbenas, some more pansies, parsley, hollyhocks, and malva. These join 'Early Girl' tomatoes, broccoli, and snapdragons, already sprouted. Weekend number nine is for main-season tomatoes, peppers, onions, fennel, and eggplant, as well as Russian statice and the first sowing of 'Victoria Blue' salvia. And so it continues down to weekend zero. Melons, cucumbers, and squash. As you can see, most of this stuff is pretty old hat, but when I try something new, I have to know where in the drawer to file the packet. Which is another reason why I like seed packets to tell me what I need to know, clearly and fully.

Over a century ago, Celia Thaxter, who sowed her Iceland poppies in empty eggshells set in boxes of sand, wrote, ". . . [I]f any seedsman would like to make his fortune without delay, he has only to have printed on every packet of seed he offers for sale the kind of soil, the food, required by each plant." Thank goodness the seedsmen were listening.

As could be expected, Burpee gives decent directions. So does Johnny's, although I dearly wish they would give them in slightly larger type. The cultural advice Pinetree offers is of the very scantiest nature. I forgive them, though, because, well, they do hit the salient points, and then there are those extremely reasonable prices. Low overhead, I guess. Almost everyone else has adequate directions, or better. Because if they don't, I'm inclined to give up on that seed house, after a while.

Not on the Thomas Jefferson Center for Historic Plants, though, despite its practice of sticking the instructions on a separate sheet *inside* the packet. But I could never give up the chance for seeds from Monticello. Besides, the back of the packet isn't filled with fluttery musings, like some I could, but won't, name. It's got interesting anecdotes about you and your relationship to the seeds within the envelope. How else do you think I found out that Bernard M'Mahon sent you the seeds of *Mirabilis longiflora* in 1812?

All in all, these are petty gripes and I really ought to desist, because, as I said, the early-spring days I spend in the nursery are unfailingly pleasurable. It's soothing and warm and insularly quiet. Just the slight crinkle of paper packets and the muted drum of watering-can rain falling on freshly sown soil. Better yet is the moment when the first seedling peers over the top of its bed. The minor annoyances vanish as completely as if they'd never existed. Before I even have time to smile in foolish wonder, the first seedling is followed by another, then by many more. Up they come, shaking off their seed hulls, reaching for the sky. Up and up. Tray after tray. A mosaic of tiny fields smelling sweetly new and tenderly green. Another garden is born and life is good.

Please accept the assurance
of my great esteem and respect,

L. Simon

Dear Mr. Jefferson

Some people were born to worry, and I am one of them. If there isn't an impending catastrophe that requires my concern, I will find an ordinary event, some more modest matter, to fret over and dwell on. My current candidate is soil. Specifically, the soil in my garden. The soil upon which the flowers, fruits, and vegetables depend for nourishment, vigor, and beauty.

Before I go any further, I ought to tell you that Jimmy doesn't understand my anxiety. Especially considering the deep, rich color of the soil and the family of fat earthworms that comes up in every shovelful. And yes, it's free of rocks, except for the bed below the strawberries, which I've always felt must be where a glacier stopped and melted down its frozen load of Pleistocene rubble. Even there, though, the soil is loamy and friable, crumbling like perfect pie crust dough when I crush a clump in my fist and then uncurl my fingers.

Most telling of all, in Jimmy's eyes, are the harvests this soil yields. The crates of ambrosial melons he trucks downtown, way too many for him to eat. The five-gallon pails of excess, ripe tomatoes, more, even, than the chickens crave. The plates heaped up with roasted asparagus, the omelets bulging with broccoli or onions. The crisp salads of green beans, snap peas, or fennel, the sweet beets that stain everything magenta. Jimmy sees the bright bouquets of flowers that fill every empty surface in the house from the end of April till October frost and scratches his head, wondering what I'm worrying about. Poor Jimmy. He just doesn't get it.

It may very well be that we cover every bed, every spring, with four or five inches of manure. Except for the potato bed, which we cover the autumn before. We occasionally lime, in the opposite season, again excluding the potato bed, and also the strawberries. Same thing with the wood ashes when Jimmy empties the stove and spreads them over the garden on a rare windless day. We sow winter rye in November and turn it in in April, and if a plant needs a boost, it gets a dose of manure tea. But here's my worry. Are we doing all of this *right*?

Has the manure reached that desirable stage reverently referred to as "well rotted"? Or are there too many shavings in it, scooping up available nitrogen as they decompose, robbing the plants? Are we liming too often? Or maybe too little? I've been told that you can't overlime, but then I've also heard, Whoa! you certainly can. Are we wasting the wood ashes by applying them in winter? Is their potassium leached away by the time the beds are planted in May?

And how about this statement from J. T. Rodale: "There is also a loss as a result of the inefficient use of manure as, for instance, when it is not applied at the season, in the manner, at the rate, or to the crop which would give the greatest return." Oh boy. And Jimmy wonders why I can't sleep at night.

It is nearly impossible these days to pick up an issue of any of the dozen or two gardening magazines flooding the market without finding some mention of the importance of soil preparation, if not an entire article devoted to the subject. Almost every book on gardening matters opens with a reminder that the soil is alive, and then proceeds with instructions for keeping it vital. Even most seed catalogs, save the truly hard-boiled, make at least a passing reference to "organic" methods of growing. Read here: Pay attention to the soil.

With all this emphasis on the soil, with these admonitions to respect its life, it no longer seems so remarkable that I'm nervous about getting it right. I could not bear to think that my soil is being "starved" or "ruined," two of the terms these books and articles brandish, right before they issue the command to add more compost. Jimmy thinks that if I stopped reading gardening magazines in bed, I'd have a more restful night. Maybe he has a point. Maybe ignorance is sleep.

As best as I can tell, the problem started in 1840 when a German chemist named Justus von Liebig published his revolutionary discovery. Plants, he said, need three elements to survive: nitrogen, phosphorus, and potassium, or NPK in chemistry shorthand. The radical part of this theory was von Liebig's assertion that plants needed *only* these three elements, that any others were superfluous. That the then existing belief in the value of humus was as laughably antiquated as the fear of falling off the edge of the earth.

No doubt he would have scoffed at your soil-management program, which called for rotating crops and fallowing fields, "aided with some manure." He probably would have considered hopelessly archaic your idea that, "The atmosphere is certainly the great workshop of nature for elaborating the fertilizing principles and insinuating them into the soil. . . . But the advantage of manuring, is that it will do more in one than the atmosphere would require several years to do. . . ."

It didn't happen overnight, but eventually von Liebig's position triumphed, ushering in the age of chemical fertilizers that still hold agriculture in their thrall today. Initially, of course, there were some old-guard holdouts, like Robert Buist, who had his own three-part formula for success. ". . . [T]he combined deposits of the horse, the cow, and the pig," he wrote in his 1847 *Family Kitchen Gardener*, were "not equalled by any or all of the nostrums of the age."

Voices like his fell silent, though, when time and Science proved von Liebig right. Plants do need nitrogen, phosphorus, and potassium for survival, but as time and Science also revealed, they can't live on these three elements exclusively. A bunch of "minor" elements are also needed, and even more "trace" elements round out the bill of fare. Magnesium, calcium, sulfur, and boron are just a few of them, sixteen elements in total.

The pity is that as Science discovered, one after another, the integral role these elements play, it didn't recommend reverting to "the great workshop of nature," where they already existed in perfect sync, but manufactured chemical substitutes instead. Obviously, this was not a time in our agricultural history when we subscribed to the notion that we should take care of the *soil*, and the *soil* would take care of the plants.

But I've already filled your ear with a lot of this stuff, so I'm not going to go over it again. The point I mean to make is that by the time my generation appeared on the scene, chemical gardening was pretty well entrenched. And even though Science is now admitting that maybe it goofed, that maybe nature has a good system after all, the general public is slower to switch gears and to break its dependence on chemical substances. Hence the spate of soil-preparation instructions. They aren't so much preaching to the already converted as they are trying to get more gardeners to see the light. They are trying to reverse decades of damage to the earth and to prevent any more from happening.

In other words, my worries are probably unfounded. I should be taking to heart the message the melons are sending, rather than second-guessing those magazine decrees. But it's still March, still raw and windy, and there are no melons to offer reassurance. In fact, nothing much at all is out in the garden, only picked-over kale, and a few carrots and parsnips, stuck in the ice-cold ground, underneath eight inches of straw.

Over in the asparagus bed, there's still no activity. The posts that will hold up seven-foot ferns, come August, are still stark skeletons rising from sodden earth. There are some stakes and a string where I planted the garlic last fall, but no sign of life in that bed, either. The cloves should be sprouting and inching their way toward light right now, but for the moment I'll just have to take their progress on faith. Same goes for the tulips, for those hundreds of bulbs. All that's visible of them is their markers. The mint looks dead and ugly in its wooden tubs, the parsley is a slimy wad, and the raspberry canes are naked.

Given this doleful scene, it's not surprising my worries are surfacing. After all, I'm trapped in the house, itching to get started, seedlings already peeking up in the nursery. What else have I got to do while I'm waiting for the weather to warm except contemplate the gardening chores ahead? And worry.

From the very first garden I ever had, back even before the zucchini and brambles, back when we were just renting a house and set a row of tomatoes beneath the bedroom window, I always used manure. In those days, I didn't know much about gardening, except that seeds sown in the ground produced plants, but somehow I knew enough to dig a liberal amount of horse manure into that ground before the sowing commenced. Maybe it was another nugget passed along from Jimmy's days in the commune in northern California, or maybe, who knows, it was even part of my family's tradition of feeding. My grandmother always felt she had failed us unless we staggered away from the table groaning with pleasure, a legacy around which my sister has built a career. Could I have felt I was offering my garden a banquet? Whatever my reason, whether subliminal or deliberate, the obvious outcome is that it worked. We grew the most delicious tomatoes I'd ever eaten, up until that time, although I've grown and eaten more delicious ones, almost yearly, since.

This whole debate about whether or not to manure, and the self-congratulations of those of us who do, probably borders on the ridiculous for someone who farmed and gardened when you did. Pre–Justus von Liebig, the continual spreading of barnyard waste was an act so common, it was taken for granted. Bernard M'Mahon, in his *American Gardener's Calendar,* barely gives manure a mention, and when he does slip it into a discussion, he certainly doesn't bother to extol its merits. There was simply the assumption that by the time you picked up his book to follow along with its month-by-month advice, this was a chore that had already been done, that was already checked off the list.

It wasn't until von Liebig came along, sowing unrest with his NPK, that thoughtful farmers and gardeners started to question their traditional methods. Whereupon they also started (dare I say it?) to worry. Were the plants getting enough nitrogen for their leaf growth? How about enough phosphorus for their roots? Or enough potassium to build stems that were sturdy? Unfortunately, the conclusion that a lot of them, starstruck by Science, came to was to dump bagfuls of inert ingredients into the ground, accomplishing their goal of feeding the plants, but in the process starving the soil. Except for the bag-of-fertilizer conclusion, you might say the same experience befell me. After my success with that first row of tomatoes and my similar luck with the patch of zucchini, I was inspired to learn more about gardening, which is when I began losing sleep.

So it is that I pass these cold, gray days wondering if I'm being kind to my soil or if I'm treating it like dirt. Do those four or five annual inches of horse manure constitute a balanced diet, or would it be more apt to call them a snack? "The manure of horses is most valued," Peter Henderson declared in *Gardening for Profit*, an 1867 release, but are all horse manures created equal, or is some of it the equivalent of canned asparagus? Take that steaming pile, hot enough to toast marshmallows, that Jimmy hauls in every spring. Does the garden find it scrumptious and nourishing, or have all the nutrients gone up with the steam?

As if the manure situation wasn't enough of a worry, next there's this business of lime. Samuel Ogden, a mid-twentieth-century convert to organic gardening, felt that once a garden was properly established, the addition of lime ceased to be necessary. Of course, in the very next sentence of his book *The New England Vegetable Garden*, Ogden admits that such a statement is "heretical," which is where my friend Steve Slosek enters the argument. Since Steve grows the best sweet corn I have ever eaten, at Moor's End Farm, down the road, when he expounds on a subject related to gardening, I'm inclined to give a listen.

The need for liming never ceases, Steve maintains, as long

as rain keeps falling from the sky. Without depressing you unduly by describing the composition of modern rain, let me merely state that it acidifies the soil. By neutralizing the acid, lime allows the plants to take up the potassium and phosphorus they need, which makes not only healthier plants but also healthier soil. "Soil is a community," Steve says, and the clusters of interacting elements it forms could almost be thought of as neighborhoods.

It's a very cozy notion until I imagine a rototiller churning through it, shattering those thriving neighborhoods like Cossacks on a raid, sending the happy denizens fleeing, driving them into hiding. Welcome to my next worry, otherwise known as soil tilth. It seems like a harmless enough term, meaning only the crumbly condition of the soil, but on closer consideration it is fraught with as many anxieties as are the considerations of lime or manure.

On the one hand, soil needs to be loosened if a garden crop is to root, but on the other hand, if the soil is pulverized, its neighborhoods plundered, it could dry up and blow away. Somewhere between the tight-knit community of unbroken earth and the fine, clean bed my cherished onions demand, a compromise must be found. Is perfect pie crust dough a tilth we can all live with?

And wait. I've barely begun. I haven't even touched on compost yet. Or on the benefits of green manure. But maybe at this point I should make another confession and tell you that I'm being a bit disingenuous, that a lot of my anxieties could be avoided. I could very easily buy one of the soil-test kits advertised in almost every catalog and magazine. Or I could send a sample of my soil to the UMass Extension Service, which would send me back an analysis, spelling out in black and white just what, if anything, my soil lacked. It would be so simple, then, to make the necessary amendments, ensuring its perfect health. Bang. Done. But if I didn't have my soil to worry about, what would I do for the month of March?

Please accept the assurance
of my great esteem and respect,

L. Simon

Dear Mr. Jefferson

It's not entirely true that I worry about my soil only because I have nothing else to do in March. I worry, also, because I'm very good at worrying. But there's something else I'm very good at, and, coincidentally, it's something else I do this month. I mean, I do it all year long, but March is when it starts. I'm talking now about my lists and charts, about my garden books. I keep excellent records.

Part of this, a goodly part, is self-defense, because my memory is so unreliable, and another part is aesthetic, because I like the sight of weathered lists and charts on clipboards hanging above the potting bench. Another part, still, is that sense of continuity I was telling you about awhile ago, the sense that my garden is history evolving, because having it all in writing connects it from year to year.

Lastly, though certainly not leastly, I enjoy keeping records because I love the tools and equipment it requires. I love pens and pencils, pads of paper, rulers, erasers, and colored markers. I love shopping for them, whether in a beautifully appointed stationery store or from the rack of a supermarket, and I love using them.

There is nothing like the heft of a Dixon Ticonderoga No. 2⅝₀ pencil. Unless, of course, it is the featherweight ease of my English rake. With its stainless-steel head and PVC shaft, it glides through those beds of manure like Hercules on skates. I

bought it through a catalog, five or six years ago, after I'd spent a few hours behind the one Dede had lent me. Last year I tried to buy another one, to have in the shed, just in case, but that catalog is now given over to selling sundials and ceramic frogs rather than the fine tools upon which its reputation was built. I have been unable to find, anywhere in the United States of America, a rake of comparable pleasure and quality. Dixon Ticonderoga No. 2$\frac{5}{10}$ pencils, on the other hand, are available from coast to coast.

Around this time every spring, I gather up those pencils and the rest of my tools and sit down at the dining room table to set up the many components that will constitute this year's garden record. Well, no, that's not entirely true, either. The map, if you remember, got made months ago, sometime last October. And at the beginning of January, on eleven by fourteen two-ply vellum bristol, I drew out this year's garden calendar. Three little rings bind its clean, open pages, month facing month, to last year's edition, identical except for the muddy fingerprints, the copious notes, and each day's square filled in with observations like "dandelions blooming" and "still picking beans." The calendar is laid out on an old dictionary stand that I bought for five dollars when the Nantucket Atheneum was renovated. It is now parked in the living room, at the foot of the stairs. Eyeglasses and pen sit on top of it, leaving no excuses for not making entries.

Also long finished is my seed-order journal, something I instituted a few years ago in a last-ditch attempt to bring some order to the chaos on the couch and a measure of relief to those three weeks of torment. It helps. Strictly speaking, it's a loose-leaf notebook of the type I always had in school, only this one is divided into Vegetables, Annuals, and Perennials, and the notes aren't about J. D. Salinger and parabolas but about exactly which varieties caught my eye and my fancy in the current issues of those nineteen catalogs, alphabetically arranged by genus and species. In theory, the usefulness of this system kicks in when I make the final orders. Instead of jumping from catalog to catalog, pawing through pages, comparing varieties and prices and numbers of seeds, I just scan through the journal and make my selections, then fill in the order blanks, calmly and confidently. In a manner of speaking.

I have another loose-leaf notebook, though this one isn't annual but ongoing. Its dividers are prepackaged a,b,c's, and in each division are my cultural hints for starting that letter's seeds. Do you recall my complaints about the paucity of instructions on some of the packets? This notebook not only fills in those gaps, it also reminds me of my previous experiences, recording those that worked as well as noting those that, alas, didn't. The sheet of plastic wrap that I always place on freshly sown verbena seeds, for example, because they need moisture to sprout but hate being watered. Or not to sow the cleome and the cosmos in the same flat, because while they both, eventually, get tall, the cosmos spring up almost overnight, but the cleome poke along for weeks.

Aside from map and loose-leaf notebooks, though, there really are two charts I set up this month. The first is to record when the seeds are sown, when they sprout, when they are transplanted, and when the seedlings move out to the cold frame, though that last column usually falls into the category of good intentions ignored. Also on this chart is an area for comments, such as my note about *Hesperis matronalis*, better known as violet sweet rocket, a wonderfully fragrant and vibrantly mauve biennial that is in bloom for weeks before anything else gets started. "Sowed once covered/once uncovered. Both sprouted. Covered seed sprouted a little better." Just goes to show. *Hesperis* supposedly needs light to germinate.

The second chart is to guide me when transplanting those seedlings, essentially telling me how many of each I need. The columns on this chart record each flower's height, color, bloom time, and imagined destination, as well as, most important, the numbers of each I transplanted for several years previously. The stern, red-inked columns and blue-inked commands are invaluable for keeping me on course at a time when the potential for derailment is great. If the chart says I need only eighteen 'Island Peppermint' petunias, then I probably don't need thirty no matter how healthy and willing those extra twelve petunias look. Conversely, if it tells me I need two hundred and eighty-eight 'Cut and Come Again' zinnias, I shouldn't give up at two hundred and forty. On the vegetable side, this chart is critical for figuring out the tomato situation, and others like it, for making sure I have enough proven varieties in case the new ones I'm trying are a big disappointment, ending up as lunch for the chickens. For remembering, too, the number of 'Sweet 100' I promised to Ken this year, and how many "grower's choice" I promised to Elin, another friend and fellow gardener.

I don't usually bother to make the Harvest List until the first "crop" is picked. In a sunny year, that would be at the end of June, and I would record how many packages of fat, red strawberries I put in the freezer. If the berries are too tart or too watery, however, as they have been for the past two miserable springs, then the Harvest List doesn't get made until early July when the peas start coming in. I'm not just compulsive about recording things. Honestly. This is another list that's really useful. Because it also has a tally of what I put up in preceding seasons, it gives me a good idea of when to stop putting up vegetables and fruits in the current one. Especially tomatoes. There are only so many meals before next summer's tomatoes are ripe.

That does it for the lists and charts, though there is one other diary of sorts I should mention. This is the spiral-bound notebook I carry into the garden, in which I figure out the distances between rows of beans, say, or draw maps of how the hot peppers are arranged. This is also the journal in which I can make notes as they immediately occur to me, and in more detail than the single slot on my charts or the small calendar box permits.

Okay. There's one more record I keep. But this is absolutely the last one, I promise. Besides, it's not really a new one but is the map from last fall, the map with quick messages jotted on the postcard-shaped beds. As each bed gets planted, in rows or grids, those dashed-off October notes become the full-fledged chronicles they hinted at. Eighty 'Sierra' potatoes were planted in two rows of forty each on May 14th. A row of 'Chianti' sunflowers, bisecting the 'Sweet 'n Early' melons, was sown on June 21st. Thirteen rows of onions went in on the fourth of June and were replaced after harvest by broccoli and kale on August 26th. By the end of the season, the map is wrinkled, creased, muddy, and faded, a document of handsome authenticity, as well as one of utilitarian accuracy.

I'm sure that a lot of people, nongardeners especially, would regard my long list of lists as cause for concern, if not outright alarm. I feel certain, though, that you would find nothing untoward about such punctiliousness, that you might even, I like to hope, find it commendable. You were a dedicated record keeper, too, taking meticulous notes when you were at Monticello and exhorting your daughters, then granddaughters, to do it in your stead when duty called you away.

"Tell me when you shall have peas, &c. up; when everything comes to table; when you shall have the first chickens hatched; when every kind of tree blossoms, or puts forth leaves; when each kind of flower blooms . . . ," you demanded of Martha in 1791, while secretary of state. Sixteen years later, from the office of president, you told your granddaughter Anne, "I wish to learn from you how the tuberoses &c. do, and particularly to have a list from you of the roots and seeds you have saved. . . ."

Your own observations were as precise as they were prodigious, filling various volumes named Farm Book, Garden Book, and Weather Memorandum Book, and spilling over to letters, ledgers, and any free-floating pieces of paper within your range. ". . . [T]he frogs had begun their song on the 7th," you wrote to Martha from Philadelphia, in March, ". . . the blue-birds saluted us on the 17th; the weeping-willow began to leaf on the 18th; the lilac and gooseberry on the 25th, and the goldenwillow on the 26th."

My favorite record, though, for the purity of its documentary spirit, for the perfection of its purpose, is "A Statement of the Vegetable market of Washington, during a period of 8. years, wherein the earliest & latest appearance of each article within the whole 8. years is noted." This vegetable timetable is a historical pearl.

How completely it captures a single fragment of activity in

our nation's capital at the outset of the nineteenth century, a fragment easily transformed into a glimpse of what life was really like nearly two hundred years ago. Not Napoleon rampaging through Europe. Not Alexander Hamilton dueled to death by Aaron Burr. But women in high-waisted dresses carrying baskets in the crooks of their arms, women holding their long skirts above the mired and rutted dirt streets of a city whose age could be measured in months. Women shopping for dinner.

Because of your "Statement," we can muse about what might have been on the menu. Asparagus, perhaps, if it was later than April 6th but before June 27th. After the asparagus went by, salsify, stewed, scalloped, or fried into cakes, might have graced Washington tables from the eleventh of June until the following April 8th. Or maybe it was broccoli, whose short season went from April 7th to the 24th. Was broccoli cooked for your birthday lunch? It seems probable that you ate broccoli, and equally probable that you enjoyed it, though I have to tell you that one of your successors, our forty-first president, has famously maligned it.

Be that as it may, I was discussing gardening records and the propensity for keeping a lot of them. This is not a unique practice by any means, at least not the act of writing things down. All those charts, tables, clipboards, and lists are another story, but gardeners have always taken notes about the doings in their gardens, and nature at large, and, more than likely, will continue to do so forever. Just as your Vegetable market "Statement" opened the curtain on an early-1800s Washington tableau, so every gardener's records open a curtain on the period in which, and the place where, the garden is growing.

In clear, neat script, James Lingard Hunter, of Randolph

County, Georgia, began his Garden Book with a list of sowing instructions, followed it with a map of his garden, and then with a string of "Frost last night" type of notes. So timeless are they, so banally familiar, I might not even have taken notice of this journal if it hadn't ended abruptly half a year after it was started. James Lingard Hunter died on June 22nd, 1846, twenty-nine years, two months, and eight days old. His garden was not an ageless one, after all, but an antebellum miasma where malaria lurked among the peach blossoms blooming in February and in the Circles of Early Peas sown in Bed No. 14.

Sarah P. Stetson, on the other hand, lived well after malaria had been conquered, and in your neck of the woods, Williamsburg, Virginia. She was a member of the Williamsburg Garden Club where her Japanese yews and her aucubas won prizes almost annually. Scotch taped between the typewritten pages of her Garden Diary, were her ribbons and awards, along with newspaper clippings, photographs, and *New Yorker* cartoons of bosomy matrons at flower shows.

The volume I have, kept from 1955 until two days after Christmas in 1969, is a charming peak at an era early in my own lifetime, an era when it was azaleas that were "gay," and when yellow alyssum and candytuft could be bought at F.W. Woolworth's, "a boon to the gardener." My memories of that now defunct five and dime store run less to the garden department and more to the lunch counter, where my mother sometimes treated me to an ice cream soda after she'd done some shopping and I'd browsed through the comic books.

But that's beside the point. Or, no, maybe it isn't. Maybe that's the point exactly. At least one of them. Without question, most of my charts and lists serve me from one year to another, reminding me of how much and how soon and how frequently, et cetera. Taken as a whole, though, maybe I'm building something else. My own pinpoint stage, maybe, with its own set of curtains. Maybe someday, forty or eighty or two hundred years hence, someone will inch back the curtains and see the Nantucket tableau posed behind them. Maybe that person, a gardener, I presume, will be amused or inspired. Or touched by sweet, personal memories hiding in the wings. What a thought. It's enough to make me reach for my ruler and sharpen another Dixon Ticonderoga No. 2$\frac{5}{10}$.

> Please accept the assurance
> of my great esteem and respect,
>
> L. Simon

Dear Mr. Jefferson

It must be that I am not sufficiently lighthearted by nature to appreciate yellow, that most cheerful of all colors, because generally speaking, I am not fond of yellow flowers, except for daffodils, of which I am. While this dispensation is probably due to the fact that daffodils are very nearly the first flowers to appear every spring, breaking the tedium of the bare branches and perennial remains we pretend add so much interest to the winter garden, I have learned that when it comes to flowers, caveats do not apply. If daffodils attain a beauty in April that I would not grant them in August, this does not diminish that beauty but is instead a lucky break for April. "To everything there is a season . . ." Especially in the garden.

What brings all this to mind is that the first daffodil opened up this morning, not one of those in a bed by the house but one on the hillside sweeping down to the stream. It's a completely yellow one, at that, yellow trumpet, yellow petals, yellow sepals, bold and bright as the rind of a lemon. This is where I'm supposed to tell you what it's called, but the truth of the matter is, I don't know its name. It might be 'Unsurpassable', but I can't be sure, because it was part of an anonymous mixture called "The Works" that I planted on the slope a dozen or more years ago. A planting that has been rewarding me with a hillside of blooms every spring since.

Daffodils, incidentally, are the one and only thing the deer will not bother. Not even a taste, as they'll take of the holly or tomatoes. After which, deciding it's not to their liking, they'll spit the fruit or foliage on the ground, a little too late, unfortunately, for the health of the plant. I have no idea why deer will bypass a daffodil, slightly toxic, to be sure, but will try, time and again, a tomato, which is, after all, a member of the deadly nightshade family. Perhaps their dislike of yellow flowers is purer than my own.

I will gladly cut this first yellow daffodil, and even more gladly cut the other unnamed varieties that come after it in lovely succession, bunching them in vases to fill the house with the color and scent of spring. And this, indisputably, is what they do, the scent brightening the house almost more than the color. I don't know how many times I've come downstairs after hours of breathing stale air in pursuit of unstale words and caught a whiff of something wonderfully fresh, something new, something thrust up from the earth. It always takes me by surprise, until I realize what it is. The daffodils.

People will often comment during January thaw that the day is so mild it could almost be spring. Sorry. Spring is not a temperature. It's a smell. Granted, mild days and sunshine help release the revivifying odors, but mild days, by themselves, don't qualify as April. In order for it to be spring, it has to smell like the grass turning green. There has to be a smell in the air of soil warming up. It doesn't hurt, of course, for there to be the sound of wrens singing, or the buzz of bees out on an exploratory flight, but in order for it to be spring, there has to be that particular, intoxicating smell, that smell that means hardy bulbs have started to bloom. Daffodils, for instance. Which are usually yellow.

Not always, however. There are also yellow and white ones, or white and yellow ones, or all-white ones, or white or yellow with accents of orange. I like all these combinations, my favorite being, usually, the one I'm looking at as I make my choice.

'Hawera', for instance, is a pretty, clear yellow whose narrow, swept-back petals give it a slightly startled look. But I also like 'Butter and Eggs', just as creamy and full as 'Hawera' is spare and pure.

Then there's one I grew for the first time last year. One that especially delighted me with its small dainty flowers of very pale, delicate yellow. Its name is 'W. P. Milner' and it came, as did 'Butter and Eggs', from an unusual company called Old House Gardens, whose owner, Scott Kunst, is a landscape historian. Some of the bulbs in his catalog date back to the 1500s, and none of them is newer than the 1920s. Let me rephrase that. The varieties are antique. The bulbs, presumably, are only a year old.

I have a couple of other sources in addition to Scott. One being John Scheepers, whose catalog has good, clear but not eye-popping, full-color photos, very helpful in making selections. Another is the Daffodil Mart, a catalog listing more than three hundred varieties, including one called 'Monticello,' which, no, I haven't bought or planted. It sounded all right, but not particularly historic, so I passed it by in favor of two wonderful whites, 'Thalia' and 'Silver Chimes', which date back to 1916 and 1914, respectively.

If you find yourself somewhat bewildered by this discussion, it's because daffodils, or perhaps I should, more properly, call them narcissi, weren't given much attention until the second half of the nineteenth century. Sure, they were grown before that, and sure, they were admired, but those were the regular old species narcissi that had been brought to England by conquering Romans and thence to America by fleeing colonists. You reported them blooming, and Bernard M'Mahon had them listed, but, again, they were never called anything more specific than Narcissus or Jonquil.

Then two Englishmen got into the act, Edward Leeds, a stockbroker by profession, and William Backhouse, a banker. Between the two of them, and a few other breeders they inspired, they had introduced a thousand varieties by the end of the century. Thirty years later, another six thousand had been bred. Today the International Daffodil Checklist names over twenty-four thousand varieties. Personally, I find that figure incomprehensible. How many variations on a daffodil can there be?

If you start with the premise, as I do, that part of the appeal of daffodils is their simplicity and tradition, then the question is begged, how many ways can you cross a daffodil before it begins to look ridiculous? I'll tell you one trick they've been made to perform that I disapprove of heartily. Some poor daffodils have been made to forfeit their trademark yellowness in order to sprout cups that are a bilious pink. Now, I like pink flowers even more than I don't like yellow ones, but pink has no business intruding on daffodil territory. Daffodils are yellow. Or else they're white. Or yellow and white. With, maybe, a splash of orange.

For hundreds of years, these flowers have been the heralds of spring. They have been as much a signal, an inseparable one, really, as that damp earth smell in announcing lengthening days. Whether nodding along roadsides or rippling across fields, whether standing primly in town gardens or spilling over the boxes beneath the chicken-house windows, daffodils mean spring is here. It's time to start gardening. That's why I like them. And why I like them yellow.

Please accept the assurance
of my great esteem and respect,

L. Simon

Dear Mr. Jefferson

It seems as though every time I write to you, I wind up regaling you with several centuries of gardening history, catching you up on a dozen or more decades of gardening developments, so I thought that, for once, you might enjoy an update that reaches back only a month. An update on my seedlings, I mean. I thought I'd give you some news from the nursery front.

Everything is doing very nicely, so far. No crop failures to remark on, though the *Malva* germinated very poorly. Perhaps this is because I bought *M. sylvestris* 'Zebrina' from Park, instead of ordering French mallow (a.k.a. *M. sylvestris*) from Monticello, which is what I usually do, and which, to my eye, is indistinguishable from the 'Zebrina'. I can't remember what my reasoning was. That was over two months ago, in another season entirely, and at a time when I was making many complex decisions rapidly, one after another. You remember my three weeks of torment, I'm sure.

The *Petunia pendula,* on the other hand, germinated with a vengeance, and now I have a mat of flat, round leaves that appears impenetrable. At the edge of their small bed, however, where the scattered seeds landed more widely, the baby *P. pendula* are four times the size of their closely packed siblings. I made a note to strew the seeds less vigorously next year or to thin them immediately, but who knows if I'll remember to read it at the appropriate moment.

I can also report that last week I did the first round of

transplanting. I've got three 'Early Girl' tomatoes and eight 'Emperor' broccoli in pots. In addition, I transplanted the number one snapdragons, 'Rocket' mix, thirty-six of them, into six-packs on the same day that I sowed seeds of 'Rocket' mix number two. I do this every year in the vain hope that I will extend the blooming period, because snapdragons are a flower that I find both elegant and droll, and because Jimmy loves to watch his bees disappear, completely, inside the dragon and to reappear, moments later, smiling, covered in pollen.

I do this succession sowing faithfully, even though the final results are slight. Number two always blooms within days of number one, if not at precisely the same time, despite being planted out at least one month apart. If I'm lucky, or if the summer is cool or the gods are benevolent, the second planting will send up an occasional stalk after the first planting is finished. Until September, that is, when those first snapdragons, having been deadheaded, produce slender side shoots, pretty enough in the garden but somewhat undernourished-looking in a bouquet.

I think I mentioned six-packs a minute ago, so I'd better explain what they are, because six-packs are a pivotal part of transplanting and transplanting is what I'm going to be doing a lot of for the next month or six weeks. Five inches square by two and a half inches deep, they are divided into six equal cells for six individual seedlings. Eight of these green plastic six-packs fit perfectly into a green plastic tray, making it a cinch to transport forty-eight plants from nursery to cold frame, then, loaded onto my Radio Flyer wagon, out to the garden.

There's another term here that probably needs explanation as well, although I don't really know what plastic is or how it is made. It's hard, but it's brittle, it's lightweight, it's smooth. It can be molded into any imaginable shape, and it never wears out, though it does scratch, rip, and break. One thing I can tell you with confidence, when you bury plastic in the soil, it doesn't turn into humus. For this reason, I try to avoid it in the normal course of life, but I'm forced to admit that plastic six-packs are the best approach to transplanting, nine times out of ten.

For that tenth time, though, I've discovered a method that's not only safer for the earth, it's healthier for the plants. Unfortunately, it's also a bit unwieldy, making it impractical for everything except the tomatoes, the melons, the zinnias, and the morning glories. If this strikes you as a curious combination, let me tell you what these four otherwise unrelated fruits and flowers have in common. For one thing, I grow all of them in just the right quantity, and for another thing, when I plant them out, I empty the tray all in one go.

These are paper pots, you see, and they come, sizes large, medium, and small, in a honeycomb of thirty, eighty, or one hundred and twenty cells, which fits into a tray, white plastic, not green, that's four inches deep. These pots have sides only, no bottoms, which makes them a little tricky to fill, but I've found that if I clip the honeycomb to the walls of the tray with clothespins before I start, the weight of the soil will hold it in place when all the cells are filled.

The beauty of this system is, first, that the roots have plenty of room to spread, and second, honeycombed together, each potful of soil stays moister, and more evenly, further good news for the roots. At planting time, this moist paper falls away like nobody's business, revealing a lovely root ball and leaving behind only a small pile of biodegradable trash. The ease with which the paper falls away is also the big drawback, however, because once you pull one plant out of the tray, all the rest want to unravel in sequence. Needless to say, this is *not* good news for the plants.

In the case of tomatoes, though, this disadvantage is negligible, because it just so happens that I grow thirty of them every year, twenty-seven for the garden and three for spares. This is not counting, of course, the ones I give to Elin and Ken or those three 'Early Girls' that I transplanted last week. Those go in the ground on the first of May, a good four weeks before the others, which wait for Memorial Day, at least.

As for the melons and the morning glories, I also grow them in a size large, thirty-cell honeycomb, though in both these cases, not all of the cells get seeded. The advantage here, however, is a therapeutic one, because melons and morning glories are both extremely touchy, and paper pots, with their fall-away sides, minimize the shock to the plants when they are removed to the ground. Fussiness is not an issue for the zinnias, but I need quantities of them at once for the hedge I make along one section of fence. Two sets of size medium paper pots, with eighty to a tray, do the deed nicely, with enough zinnias left over to stick into tubs by the back porch and the chicken-house door.

These are the exceptions, though. Six-packs are the norm. With a parenthetical mention of four-packs, which are six-packs' green plastic cousins. Into these go seedlings that get larger faster, dahlias, for example, or balsam, or hot peppers, or cosmos, or cleome, if I can ever get the seeds to germinate. For plants that need more growing room still, like broccoli, or eggplant, or pumpkins and squash, there are individual pots, four inches square and three and a half inches deep. What all these containers share is their green plastic composition, that stuff that doesn't decompose when buried in the earth. That's the rub.

Since I can't, in good conscience, toss out this plastic at the end of the season, I store it away every winter and pull it out every spring. That means hosing down each piece to flush away old, caked debris, then tossing it into a vat of water and bleach to kill off any unwelcome bacteria. I can state, unequivocally, that this whole process is a colossal nuisance.

First of all, I have to dress for the occasion. Rubber boots, rubber gloves, and rubber bib overalls. Then, although I always aim for a day that's sunny and windless, in Nantucket that serendipitous weather confluence occurs approximately once every other April. As a result, I find myself chasing six-packs all over the lawn, stumbling along after them in my clumsy fisherman's garb.

As an excellent example of how everything is relative, I must tell you that this tiresome chore is a veritable joy as compared with the other annual job in which bleach is also employed. For this job, I take everything out of the shanty, then scrub it down, floor, ceiling, and walls. The shanty, so you know, is a little gray-shingled shed that Jimmy built when he fished, every winter for seventeen years, for bay scallops, those from Nantucket being the sweetest and most delicate in the world.

Since the scallops have to be cut from their shells before they can be sold, Nantucket is dotted with shanties where scallops are opened. Most shanties, and ours is no exception, have heat, hot and cold running water, and strong, built-in benches with waterproof surfaces. The perfect potting shed, in other words. Just add some simulated sun.

Because my baby seedlings—remember them back in the nursery?—like all babies, grow up quickly. First they get taller and start making new leaves, then, how time flies, they start clamoring for real food and, soon after that, a room of their own. That's when they move out to the shanty, which, unlike the guest room, never changes its name, even though its days of scallop opening are over and done. It's also when the seedlings take up residence in those green plastic six-packs, but before any of this happens, their new quarters have to be washed out and sterilized.

Once these distasteful tasks are behind me, I can settle into the pleasure of transplanting. I say pleasure, knowing it will raise eyebrows all over the island. Whenever I visit Bartlett's or Moor's End Farm in the spring, everyone is standing with their hands in piles of potting mix, glassy-eyed and yawning. But they are transplanting hundreds, maybe thousands, of the same plant or variety, while I am transplanting a couple or three dozen of each, a flat or two at the most. Not counting the zinnias, of course. It gives me the chance to know every seedling person-ally, to tsk over the tiny ones and to cluck with pride over the giants. To admire their wee roots and to imagine how they'll look a few months down the road.

Sometimes baby plants, as is the case with baby people, look exactly as they will in maturity, only in miniature. Other times, while a few basic features are recognizable, adulthood reshapes them into an entirely different image. In the former category, marigolds are what comes immediately to mind. Even at the transplant stage, they are precise little replicas of their grown-up selves, sturdy and stout, with dark green, almost fernlike foliage. This engaging lack of guile is one of the reasons I like them, even though their flowers are frequently yellow, and yellow at its brassiest.

I'm speaking about the dwarf French marigolds, I should add, about the 'Sophias', the 'Janies', the 'Heroes', the 'Boys'. I don't care as much for the taller American varieties, because I've found that most of them tend to lose their crisp appearance by August and to get ratty on the bottom. Nor do I like white marigolds, a hybrid Burpee spent decades developing. Their efforts to do so make an interesting story, which I'll tell you sometime, but the flower that resulted is, for my money, uninspired. Marigolds, like daffodils, I feel, were meant to be yellow. Or else orange. Or rust.

As long as I'm complaining, I might as well say that I also disapprove of the attempts being made to breed a marigold without its traditional odor. This is a heresy. I know that some people, and rabbits, allegedly, find the smell of a marigold repugnant, but I don't happen to be one of them. To me, marigold scent is another one of those garden signposts, again, like daffodils, only instead of heralding spring, this one is a constant of summer. Now that I think about it, it's probably this scent that endears the marigold to me, even more than how cute it looks in six-packs on the bench of the shanty.

While I'm at it, I should give you an example of a plant in the latter category, of a plant whose baby features change shape as it ages. I've got a dandy one in nemophila, which sounds more like a psychic disorder than a flower, though that's what it is, making a saucy white cup with purple blue markings. From its first set of true leaves until it reaches maturity, nemophila is so adorable I want to hug it to my bosom. Its long, strong little leaves have such a pert, picot-edged frill, the seedlings seem like paper doll cutouts, the ones that cavort after midnight while the human world sleeps. Sad to say, this youthful buoyancy gives way, in adulthood, to foliage that is, while still frilled, merely droopy and messy. At least it is for me, here in Nantucket.

This leads me to another interesting issue, because those nemophila—'Five Spot' is their name—came from a packet of seeds I picked up one time when I was in England. I'm sure you've heard that, since your day, we've mended our differences with our former oppressor. Indeed, we've become the best of buddies. So much so, as far as gardening is concerned, that we've been falling all over ourselves for scores of years trying to duplicate the gardens of Surrey, and Sussex, and the Cotswold cottages.

"The gardening in that country [England] is the article in which it surpasses all the earth," you wrote after a 1786 visit, suggesting, perhaps, that American infatuation with English gardening goes back several centuries at least. Although you were referring to the grounds surrounding the great manors you toured, and not to the cozy, color-splashed borders that are currently capturing our fancy.

I'm not saying that this adulation is misplaced. Good gracious no. English gardens are a marvel to behold, but for as many years as we've been trying to re-create them on this side of the Atlantic, there's been one lonely voice or another crying out that you can't grow English gardens in an American climate. Apparently, not even nemophila in Nantucket.

But I digress. Again. And after I promised I wouldn't talk about anything more than one month old. So back to transplanting, which begins in earnest this week. Not that I'm through sowing seeds, not by a long shot. After all, this is only weekend number six and there are still plenty of packets in the drawer awaiting their turns. There's still a week at least before anything can be put out in the cold frames, the last stop for seedlings before they get planted in the garden. It's early times yet, but it won't be for long.

There comes a moment, usually around the middle of May, when I'll run out of space to make another move. Both big cold frames will be full, as will the auxiliary one Jimmy built a few years back. The two shanty benches will be cheek by jowl with trays, even crossing over the flimsy, one-legged bridge on the far wall. Upstairs, in the nursery, the situation will be the same. Too many trays, not enough room. It will still be too early to set anything but the hardiest plants in the garden, so the stalemate will continue for a week or ten days.

But that's a month away. For now, I can sit on my stool at the end of the bench, teasing tiny seedlings out of their nursery beds and planting them in six-packs. Poke a hole in each cellful of potting mix with my index finger, lower down the root threads, pack the soil around them snugly. Over and over and over again. Label the six-packs with a sliver of a tongue depressor, mark the charts lined up on the wall in front of me. Date and quantity and any remarks.

Outside the shanty, the day is sometimes sunny, but this is April in Nantucket, so frequently it isn't. And the wind. Always the wind. Blowing off the Atlantic Ocean, it is still tinged with winter. Inside, though, the air is comfortable and moist, balmy from the heater and the trays of small, green plants growing in warm, damp soil. Poke a hole, lower down a seedling, pack it in tightly. Breathe in the smells of baby marigolds and tomatoes and basil. Outside the shanty, spring might be reluctant, but inside the shanty I'm inching toward summer. One seedling at a time.

Please accept the assurance
of my great esteem and respect,

L. Simon

Dear Mr. Jefferson

Since the Dutch first went nuts over tulips in 1634, untold miles of words have been written in praise of these splendid flowers and on the pleasure they bring to gardeners every spring, starting right about now. For sheer bliss, however, for unaffected rapture, I don't think I've ever read a passage as touching as the one written by your granddaughter Ellen.

"The roots arrived," she wrote, describing her childhood memories of Monticello, "labelled each one with a fancy name. There was Marcus Aurelius, and the King of the Gold Mine, the Roman Empress, and the Queen of the Amazons, Psyche, the God of Love, etc., etc., etc. Eagerly, and with childish delight, I studied this brilliant nomenclature, and wondered what strange and surprisingly beautiful creations I should see rising from the ground when spring returned, and these precious roots were committed to earth under my grandfather's own eye . . . Then, when spring returned . . . what joy it was for one of us to discover the tender green breaking through the mould, and run to grandpapa to announce, that we really believed Marcus Aurelius was coming up, or the Queen of the Amazons was above ground! . . . Then when the flowers were in bloom, and we were in ecstacies over the rich purple and crimson, or pure white, or delicate lilac, or pale yellow of the blossoms, how he would sympathize with our admiration. . . ."

Although it might not mean as much to her, I can certainly

sympathize, too. I am tremendously glad to see the daffodils, every April, brightening the hillside down to the stream, but this gladness is nothing beside the deep sense of awe and exultation that the tulips inspire. They are very nearly perfect flowers, to my mind, exquisitely simple of shape, their beauty carried by the luxurious texture of their petals and by the array of their colors, each one as clean and pure as anything Nature can design.

Well, no, that's not exactly true. There are a few tulips that I find unfortunate. Take 'Jimmy', for example. How thrilled I was to discover him on the pages of the McClure & Zimmerman catalog a few years ago, for reasons that I don't think require explanation. I ordered him in July, planted him in November, and spent all winter anticipating his bloom. What a disappointment! He came up tall and strong, a healthy-looking plant, but the color of his flower was a vile hue, somewhere between mustard and mud. 'Jimmy' the tulip was dispatched, forthwith, to the compost heap, though I'm happy to report that the other Jimmy is still a garden fixture.

To be completely candid, the McClure & Zimmerman catalog was not my first acquaintance with 'Jimmy', although it has been for other, more gratifying selections, the raspberry sherbet 'Gander's Rhapsody', to name one. Actually, I first bumped into 'Jimmy' at Keukenhof Gardens, an immaculate and impressive exposition of tulips in Lisse, Holland. It's no coincidence that Keukenhof is the world's largest showcase for tulips, or that Lisse is its location, because Holland is the world's largest producer of tulips, and Lisse is smack-dab in the middle of the Tulip District. From this comparatively tiny area, a dike away from the North Sea, come nine *billion* spring-blooming bulbs, give or take, every year, the majority of which are tulips.

As spectacular as Keukenhof is, however, and where 'Jimmy', incidentally, was an appealing shade of mango, for a truly intoxicating tulip experience you have to see the bulb fields. For openers, it's necessary to drive by them in a car, to see the arrow-straight bands of reds, yellows, pinks, purples, and whites, stretching across paper-flat fields, until they disappear on the horizon. At high speeds, these bands of vivid color flash by like sun through a prism, or a deck of rainbows being shuffled.

Follow this up with a walk through a field, preferably on a day when the wide Dutch sky is the same blue as Delft china. Other nice touches are a few fat cows placidly grazing off in the distance, or perhaps a windmill, or a thatch-roofed farmhouse, or a silvery thread of canal. Especially effective is a nearby field of hyacinths in bloom, their fragrance hanging like syrup in the chill North Sea breeze.

The main event, though, is the tulips themselves. Hundreds of them. Thousands of them. Shoulder to shoulder, head to head. Four rows to a band, each band one meter wide, and band upon band of one variety only. 'Douglas Baader', say, a pretty, pleasing pink, or clear white 'Maureen', or the yellow and red 'Keizerkroon', first introduced in 1750 and still popular today.

There aren't many tulips in that last category, by the way. New varieties are being bred so fast and furiously that the varieties that came before them fall by the wayside, barely remembered. Then again, our tastes are continually changing, a fact that the tulip breeders haven't failed to keep pace with. Not the successful ones, anyway.

After that whole frenzy of Tulipmania got squelched, the Dutch settled down to some serious bulb production. What they set their sights on were the tulips that were artfully streaked by disease, a happenstance referred to as "broken" and an effect much coveted by seventeenth- and eighteenth-century gardeners, including, from all indications, you. Today these broken tulips are considerably less esteemed, and the ones that pop up are "rogued," or unceremoniously yanked from the fields and destroyed. Today, for the most part, we prefer unblemished colors, or else ones that are subtly infused, like 'Apricot Beauty', probably America's favorite. Its name says it all; I don't think I need to describe it.

This whole shift in tulip taste began, as did so many gardening trends, with the Victorians, this one born of their love of "bedding out" masses of flowers. Until the Victorians came along, tulips were displayed either as single specimens or in the small collections you seemed to favor, giving individual appearance more importance than overall effect. One letter that reached you in the White House in 1808 reported that all your flowers were "coming up very well," including the tulips, of which "forty flourishing ones" were counted. This number would not have impressed a gardener at the other end of the century, who ordered tulip bulbs by the hundred lot for eighty cents or a dollar. 'Keizerkroon' cost two.

Standing in the middle of thousands of tulips, it's easy to appreciate this passion for bedding, although I suspect it's more stunning as bands across a flat field in Holland than as the centerpiece of a recently mowed lawn. A Dutch bulb field excites a certain greed, a surreptitious desire. There are so many tulips, each one so perfect, so beautifully shaped, so fresh, so gleaming. You want to fill your eyes with more tulips and more tulips and then even more. To touch them, or to brush them against your lips. The fine nap of their petals seems part beeswax, part velvet, all of it luscious.

Of course, you have to time this excursion correctly, because two days after they bloom, the tulips are decapitated. That's right. Their heads are snapped off and thrown in a heap, then the cows are let in for a colorful feast. All that's left is bands of green foliage and naked stems. Fields full of broad tulip leaves ripening as summer approaches. Heartbreaking as this practice is, I suppose I understand it, albeit grudgingly. The object of the exercise is to make huge, healthy bulbs, so that the gorgeous flowers can bloom later, in my garden and yours.

That's probably why tulip merchants have nothing to fear from my bulb-saving routine. I don't cut off the flowers until the petals are mottled and desiccated. While this method allows me to enjoy the blooms to the last moment of their beauty, and beyond it, it most emphatically is not conducive to what is known in the industry as "top-sized" bulbs. In fact, each year my tulips get weenier and the flowers they produce get increasingly pathetic. They might do as bright spots of color, viewed from a distance, but for the tulips I cut or admire close up, they aren't nearly fat and beautiful enough. Which is how it came to be that every July 21st, I pass my birthday in the rocking chair on the porch, thumbing through bulb catalogs, filling in order blanks, buying myself presents.

Come the end of April, I need to see tulips in bloom. Specifically 'Sweetheart' and 'Couleur Cardinal', with the lovely, double white 'Schoonoord', ready to burst. 'Sweetheart' is yellow, a creamy yellow with a faint ribbon of ivory around the edges, beloved, despite this drawback, for its early appearance and its habit, when cut, of splaying open its cup and swelling to the size of a salad plate. Set on a windowsill with the sunshine behind it, 'Sweetheart' is sensational enough to make my knees go weak. Even the stamens, falling off one by one, are beautiful, like burnt paper matches, sooty and black.

The only thing better than this bouquet is when a few stalks of 'Couleur Cardinal' join 'Sweetheart' in the vase. The irony here is that red is another color I'm not usually drawn to, but 'Couleur Cardinal', another early tulip and another unshakable favorite, is so diligently red, it nearly turns purple with the effort. Introduced in 1845, it is also one of the oldest named tulips on the market, with only 'Keizerkroon', and possibly the rose and white 'Zomerschoon', being older. I say possibly, because while 'Zomerschoon', introduced in 1620, undeniably predates 'Keizerkroon' by a hundred and thirty years, its presence in commerce is not as certain. Scott Kunst, at Old House Gardens, is hot on its trail, and as soon as he offers it, 'Couleur Cardinal' will slip back a notch. In record books only, not in my garden.

Almost as old, going back to 1860, is a tulip called 'Van der Neer', a plum purple beauty. This is one tulip I grow not in the garden but close to the house, taking my chances with the rabbits, who remain a threat despite the winter fence I've finally learned to put up. Some years they win, some years I do. When it's my turn, the show 'Van der Neer' puts on makes it worth the risk. I have it planted next to 'King of the Blues' hyacinths and in front of a 'China Boy' holly. The fragrance is a knockout, but so are the rich, striking colors.

Colors need to be strong in the spring. They need to stand up to the high, bright sun and against the emerald blue of the cold Atlantic. Spring is a rugged season, only barely taming the harshness of winter, a vehement season with a touch of danger. That's why, in spring, it takes deep, emphatic colors to stir my blood.

Of course, these could be my New England roots showing. Spring in Virginia might be gentle and sweet, pastels more appropriate. But tulips don't have a southern heritage, at least not recently. They come from the Netherlands, on the North Sea, and before that Vienna, and before that, half a millennium ago, from the courts of Constantinople. Yes, that was a more temperate climate, but take notice, please, none of those tulips are around today, never mind for sale.

That's why I'm not telling you about 'Don Quichotte', and 'Atilla', 'General Eisenhower', and the rest, because even though they thrill me today, they may vanish tomorrow. 'Van der Neer', 'Keizerkroon', 'Couleur Cardinal', and remember 'Clara Butt' from 1889? They've been around awhile. They've stood the test of time. Their trails aren't going to peter out in floral history anytime soon.

Which brings me back to Ellen and her "brilliant nomenclature." 'Marcus Aurelius', 'King of the Gold Mine', etc., etc., etc., have disappeared without a trace. I have looked for them everywhere I could think of and have even enlisted Scott Kunst in the search. Nothing doing. He turned up a 'Psyche', but it probably wasn't yours. This 'Psyche' didn't make her debut until around 1900. And no sign of her now.

Bernard M'Mahon, who is frequently quite helpful, names not a single variety in his *American Gardener's Calendar*, though he does go into detail on tulip classes and divisions. Primo Baguets had white flowers streaked with brown. Incomparable Verports had cups "which are very handsome." These, along with Bybloemens, Bizards, and Baguet Rigauts, he took "the liberty of requesting your acceptance of" in 1806. It probably won't surprise you to learn that this isn't the way things are set up now. Today the predominant tulip classes are Triumphs and Darwins, along with Early and Late Singles and Doubles, although the Bybloemens are still around and the Bizards have become Bizarres.

All of which goes to prove, once again, that a garden is both timeless and changing, that it's history on the move, the past and the future combining. I'll probably never know what "strange and surprisingly beautiful creations" broke the mould and brought Ellen so much joy. I could speculate, of course. I could cobble together clues. But in the end it would be just a guess, while there *is* one thing I know for sure. The joy. Ellen's joy, her wonder and delight, her ecstasies over the blooms are as enduring as tulips themselves.

I can say this with confidence because I have just picked the first bunch of 'Sweetheart' tulips and set them in a jar on the sill. Pretty soon they'll open up and the sun will shine through their petals, creamy yellow, like beeswax and velvet. If that isn't ecstasy, I don't know what is.

Please accept the assurance
of my great esteem and respect,

L. Simon

Dear Mr. Jefferson

The first asparagus came to table today.

Oh boy. I've been waiting for months to write those words. Not only in anticipation of the asparagus, more of which in a minute, but also because I love this phrase, "came to table." I find it enticing and evocative, conjuring up images both delicious and grand. You don't see it used much these days, and no modern equivalent has sprung up to take its place. There is no similar, single phrase that states its case with such clarity and grace, no phrase that so perfectly entwines the acts of eating and dining.

Perhaps this is because these two acts are, all too often today, not entwined. Eating is something that's done in a hurry, standing at the kitchen counter or off a tray in front of the television. Note the absence of tables in these scenes. (And please don't ask me about television.) Tables in too many homes are sat around and dined at only a few times a year, most conspicuously at Thanksgiving, and Christmas, and if there happens to be company—none of these occasions, as a general rule, coinciding with the first appearance of vegetable crops, much less those picked fresh from the garden. Come to that, many people don't even know that there are seasons for vegetables, because all vegetables are available all year in the produce departments of supermarkets, flown in from whatever corner of the planet happens to be experiencing the season required.

I'm not going to admit where we stand, or sit, on the issue

of dining, but I will say that when it comes to eating, our meals are definitely tied to the seasons. Part of this is garden altruism, I suppose, but most of it is flavor. Supermarket vegetables that have made the journey from Chile, or Mexico, or even California don't bear any resemblance to the ones that grow in my garden. Over time, we have gradually arrived at the point where we gorge ourselves during each vegetable's prime, put it by if that's an option, and otherwise wait for it to come around again. I realize that this way of eating is hardly worth mentioning to someone of your era, but, believe me, in this day and age, we're regarded as weird. We have the last laugh, though. Not only are all our meals wonderfully good, we also get to indulge our cravings with gluttonous binges.

Which brings me back to asparagus, an outstanding example of this wholly satisfactory dietary regime, being a vegetable we eat for only six, or maybe eight, weeks every year, but when it's those weeks of the year, we *really* eat asparagus. It's the main course for dinner three nights out of seven, and on the nights it's not the entrée, half a dozen or so spears are apt to show up in the salad. Or the risotto, or the soup.

Fearing Burr, in the 1865 edition of his authoritative *Field and Garden Vegetables of America,* recommends boiling young shoots for "twenty minutes or half an hour, until they become soft. . . . ," then serving them on toast with melted butter, further evidence, I feel, that seedsmen should stick to cultural tips and leave recipes to cookbooks. It's not the toast and melted butter I object to, in fact I may try it that way before this season is over, but I must protest boiling asparagus for any length of time, let alone for half an hour. If the shoots are truly young, a minute or two of steaming is all they need, more than enough time to turn shamrock green and shiny, each bite sublimely tender. As a further bonus, none of their flavor is boiled away, and all their vitamins are retained in the bargain.

Even better than steaming, though, my method of choice is peeling the spears, rubbing them in olive oil, sprinkling them with coarse salt, then roasting them in the oven until their buds get slightly crunchy and their stalks are like cream. Put a pile of this asparagus on a plate and put a poached egg on top of it, and the meal that results is savory and succulent beyond the breadth of my vocabulary to describe it. Especially if those spears have been cut from the garden moments before roasting, the same moments that the eggs were rushed in from the henhouse. These eggs, poached, break over the top of the asparagus pile, their plump, orange yolks making a sauce so rich and smooth, the most haut French chef would give all his stars to achieve it. We eat this meal a lot during asparagus season and never get bored. It is devoured with as much pleasure at the end of June as it is on May 2nd.

Apart from the differing culinary approaches, very little has changed since you first sowed asparagus seeds in 1767, indeed since the Romans grew and prized it, several centuries B.C. Before we leave the subject of eating it, entirely, I think it's worth noting that Emperor Augustus was allegedly fond of saying, *"Citius quam asparagi coquentur,"* which they tell me means, "Do it quicker than you can cook asparagus." This seems to indicate that asparagus wasn't always boiled indefinitely in the manner Fearing Burr describes, though to give him his due, a recipe in *The Virginia Housewife,* first published in 1824, gives essentially identical directions. The author of the cookbook, quite famous in its day, was Mary Randolph, who, I think I've figured out, was your daughter's sister-in-law, Martha's husband being her brother. Your contemporary, anyway.

Mary Randolph does admonish cooks to keep a careful eye on the pot and to pull asparagus out at "the exact time of their becoming tender." This advice leads me to believe that either the early-nineteenth-century ideal of vegetable tenderness was far mushier than our modern one or else the asparagus was tougher. Probably some of both, leaning more heavily toward the latter.

It's hard to know for sure how asparagus itself has changed, because none of the varieties M'Mahon listed in his *Catalogue* are extant for a taste test today. The same is true of the two named varieties in your Garden Book, 'East India', which you recorded sowing, and 'Cooper's pale green', which you received as a gift. Throughout the rest of the century, other varieties came and went, never a vast selection but always five or six. Of those, only two, 'Conover's Colossal' and 'Argenteuil', the pride of France, are still clinging to existence, although just barely. Then there's Peter Henderson, as respected as they came, who maintained that . . . "the *Asparagus officinalis* of our gardens is confined to only one variety," that any variations were only those wrought by differences in climate. Hmm.

I guess what happened in the twentieth century is the biggest news in asparagus culture since Pliny the Elder. First came the Washingtons and then came the Jerseys, both of which really were different. The Washington varieties were introduced around 1918 by the United States Department of Agriculture, though what with World War I and then the Great Depression, it took awhile for them to catch gardeners' attention. By the 1940s, however, 'Mary Washington' was the queen of the patch, or of the "asparagus plantation," as M'Mahon would have put it. In addition to being reliable and prolific,

'Mary Washington' offered the first real resistance to rust, a big problem with the older varieties. Or variety, if you concur with Peter Henderson.

'Mary Washington', and 'Martha Washington', to a lesser degree, as well as a few others in the Washington family, dominated the field for a good half century. Then, in New Jersey, at Rutger's University, a whole new strain of asparagus was bred and introduced, beginning in 1985. 'Jersey Knight', 'Jersey Giant', and 'Jersey King', to name the main ones, solved an even bigger problem plaguing asparagus growers, that of female plants using all their energy to make seed-bearing berries instead of edible spears. The Jerseys are all male, a rare instance where that aggregation is desirable, the Red Sox starting lineup being the only other one that springs immediately to mind.

In my asparagus plantation, now ten years old, there were originally two rows of 'Mary Washington' and one of 'Jersey Knight'. It was one of the Mary's that Dede and I replaced, because the 'Jersey Knight' was outproducing both other rows by astronomical amounts. If we had to rely solely on 'Mary Washington', we would either have to quintuple the plantation or go without binges. Not a pleasant prospect.

There are, I suppose, two other changes in asparagus cultivation I should mention. The first one is salt, the second is blanching. Up until the turn of this century, both were considered not only beneficial but necessary. The salt as a fertilizer, the blanching for flavor.

I'm not sure how the salt thing got started, but everyone, through the ages, recommended it highly. "Salt is an excellent manure for Asparagus," said James L. Vick, giving voice to the general sentiment. Nor am I exactly sure how the theory got debunked. Science, I suppose. It was finally realized that asparagus is extremely tolerant of salt, and it thrives by the coast, but that doesn't mean that the gardener needs to add "one quart of salt to each square rod" of garden, as D. M. Ferry suggested. Just manure. Horse manure, that is. Lots and lots of it.

The business of blanching falls under the heading of food fashions, I think. Somehow white asparagus picked up the reputation for being more refined, an issue that caused divisiveness and controversy among asparagus fanciers. In his classic 1901 treatise, *Asparagus,* F. M. Hexamer does a marvelous job of encapsulating the two opposing camps. He quotes Professor Du Pre, of Clemson Agricultural School, scorning white asparagus as "tasteless, insipid," while praising the green, "into which the sunshine has put the flavor of ambrosia. . . ."

On the other side of the argument is Monsieur Leboeuf, a famous French asparagus expert, who defended the white as "more tender and delicate." He further asserted, with typical Gallic aplomb, that "To serve up green asparagus is to dishonor the table." There's that table again.

I know you are a great admirer of French tastes, especially *de cuisine*, so very possibly you are in the camp that likes its asparagus white. I would be letting you down, therefore, if I failed to report that fresh, white asparagus, today, in America, is quite difficult to find. It's still around in cans. People buy it for canapés. I've had it. It tastes like the tin can plus the brine that it's sitting in, hardly even a food, never mind asparagus, "King of the Vegetables." No, we'll take our asparagus green, roasted, and even though it deserves the honor of a table, we usually consume it, with no less relish, seated at the marble counter in the kitchen that was supposed to be for making pastry.

Really, these are slight changes, fluctuations, more accurately, when you consider the long history of asparagus cultivation. Plant them in trenches, well prepared with manure, then top-dress them annually, and big, stout asparagus will rise out of the earth for a score of years, or more, regular as clockwork. On this everyone is agreed.

Of course, a bit of patience is required initially. You can't cut any asparagus for the first year or the second. The third year you can cut lightly, the fourth year you can gorge, and this, too, is the way it's been since time immemorial. Six or eight weeks has always been the season. F. M. Hexamer says the old rule of thumb is to cease cutting "when green peas are abundant. . . ." I have to modify that rule here on our ocean-chilled island, where I don't have peas until the beginning of July. Here in Nantucket, our last meal of asparagus usually ends with our first bowl of strawberries.

Perhaps this is why asparagus and strawberries are linked in my mind. Why I think of them as the first two crops to come to table, be that table figurative or literal. A statement in itself that's a little misleading, because we eat plenty of other meals from the garden before the first strawberry is ripe. To back up a bit, up as far as April, there are the leftovers from what I planted last summer and fall.

The kale, to cite one, puts out new leaves early in the spring, pale ones, almost yellow on the green varieties, lavender-veined on the 'Red Russian'. They are, of course, getting ready to go, spectacularly, to seed, but in the meantime, those new leaves are unimaginably tender and sweet, while still a touch spicy. Then there are the carrots, juicier now than they were in August. Ditto the parsnips, the size of butternut squash, but absolutely superb puréed with the last of the leeks.

After this stuff is pulled, so the beds can be dressed, there's a short wait until the new round begins. Leading the parade, as I've already said, is the asparagus, but not too long after it, the sorrel is ready for soup. Then it's June and quite a bit comes in, mustard and spinach, naturally, and the first head of the broccoli. We start eating big salads for dinner, with hard-boiled eggs, salads made with 'Tennis Ball' lettuce, planted in your honor, and 'Susan's Red Bibb', planted for my sister. And radishes and arugula. By the end of the month, if we're lucky, there are a few leaves of chard, and, if we're really lucky, there may be a fennel.

About this time, the strawberries commence. They aren't as predictable as the asparagus, in either timing or taste. While the asparagus emerge from the dark depths of the earth seemingly immune to what's happening on the surface, the strawberries tie their fates to our unreliable spring weather. They want sunshine to make them fat and red and sweet, a condition I can't promise them, would that I were able.

Among the carefully kept records I so admire are your observations, over a seven-year period, of the ripening date of strawberries at Monticello, "nearly central to" Virginia. Between 1810 and 1816, the first strawberries came to table from May 3rd to May 25th. My own records on this matter are more scattershot, particularly since, in my garden, there is a gap between the date I first pop a red strawberry into my mouth and the date, usually a week or more later, when a respectable quantity of them are ripe all the way through and ready to be picked. There's no telling about the former date, but this latter one rarely falls before the last week in June.

Even without looking it up, I can tell you when I always hope it will happen. I always hope I'll have a picking by Hilda's birthday, on June 25th. It was always my wish that I could serve strawberries for dessert, either the classic and enduringly wonderful strawberry shortcake or, if the harvest was light, as a garnish on a carrot cake, another *specialità della casa.*

Lobster came first, another favorite of Hilda's. Susan took charge of cooking it, provided, of course, she was on island, which she usually tried to be. Aunt Evelyn tried to be here, too, and frequently was, and once or twice Aunt Jessie also made it. They were Hilda's sisters, Jessie the older one, Evelyn the younger.

Hilda is gone now, and Aunt Jessie is bedridden in Florida. Aunt Evelyn still visits regularly, but for my birthday in July, or Jimmy's in September, which, incidentally, is Nantucket's most glorious month. What can I say? Lives change. The people you love the most dearly die. In their aching absence you hang onto memories, to moments, to locks of hair. Me, I keep wishing for enough strawberries to make dessert, by June 25th.

The strawberries I wish for would be almost unrecognizable to you, I think. Maybe blindfolded you'd guess, sniff test only. Your strawberries were tiny, "100 fill half a pint," you measured, and I'm willing to bet they were wildly flavorful. Berries today have swollen dramatically. Some of the ones in my garden, as I once remarked, are as big as Roger's paw. And those aren't even the large varieties. There are some strawberries on the market the size of apples, grown commercially for dipping in chocolate.

With this growth, unfortunately, has come a proportional loss of flavor. Forget about those huge ones. They taste like the chocolate they're dipped in. Strawberries have been hard hit by marketabilityitis, that syndrome of breeding fruits and vegetables for their shipping endurance, for their flawless appearance, and for their efficiency of culture. Being such a soft fruit, essentially skinless (and a member of the rose family, which I find quite fitting), you can imagine how much the breeders have had to fiddle with strawberries to bring them up to spec.

This isn't to say that today's strawberries, when grown in good rich soil and allowed to ripen fully on the stem, aren't awfully delectable. They are. No doubt about it. There are, in fact, few more sensual gardening pleasures than squatting in the strawberry bed, stuffing berries in my mouth, the early summer sun flushing the bare skin on my face, arms, and legs, the earth still cool beneath my naked toes. The strawberries, warmed to the consummate height of their flavor, stain my fingers and lips before they slide, juicy and smooth, down my throat. This is one of the moments worth living for. The thing of it is, though, it could be better.

Before you brand me a malcontent, let me quickly add that it's only by chance that I can say this with authority. If it weren't for two separate experiences, twenty-five years apart, I might well be squatting in my strawberry bed, fingers and mouth red, barefoot, ignorant, and happy. Happier.

The first experience was in Italy, as so many were, way back, my first summer, when I was a wide-eyed American abroad. It happened in Mantua, an exquisite, small Renaissance city, where the Palazzo Ducale is full of stunning frescoes by Andrea Mantegna. I have to sidetrack a minute, because I think you'll enjoy this. I have to tell you that the Palazzo Ducale was the home of the Gonzaga family.

One of them, Ludovico, was a letter writer of prolificacy rivaling your own, and his subject matter, frequently, was agricultural concerns. Like you, he was often away, tending to matters of state, not in Philadephia or Washington, of course, but in Venice and elsewhere. Also like you, he collected things for the garden and forwarded them home, once, in 1448, sending his wife, Barbara, a box of melon seeds with instructions to plant them. I got this last information from a book by Roger Swain, a biologist, excellent writer, and television Victory Gardener. He, apparently, got it from his wife, a Renaissance scholar.

Firsthand, though, I can tell you about my experience in Mantua five hundred and twenty years after Ludovico sent melon seeds to Barbara. It was a gorgeous July day, the sky was deep blue and cloudless, and we had just come out of the Palazzo Ducale, Susan and I and the Italian friend who'd brought us there, heads reeling from the beauty of Mantegna's paintings. The Italian friend took us to lunch at a trattoria in town. We sat outside, under a grape arbor, and ate something, probably wonderful, I don't remember what. Then came dessert.

In a plain glass bowl, without embellishments or hyperbole, was a mound of tiny strawberries, *fragole di bosca*, picked in the woods that morning and still damp from the dew. I ate every one of them. I couldn't believe anything tasted that good. Seeing our enjoyment, our friend ordered another round for the table, and I gobbled every one of those up, too. I could have eaten another bowlful, but discretion demanded I decline the third. How can I describe it? The flavor was intense. Every tiny bite was strawberry quintessence.

Go forward this time only twenty-five years, to my garden in Nantucket and my strawberry bed. There was always one row that tasted leagues better than the others, but it took me several seasons to figure out why. At first I thought it was a coincidence, then I posited that being on the outside, it got more sun. Then I thought it was because the crowns were younger, a valid theory, until even younger ones fruited. That's when I realized that the outstanding strawberries were a variety called 'Fairfax'.

"Naw," Jimmy said when I told him of this discovery.

"Yeah?" he said, having another handful.

"Yes," he said, squatting down in the bed.

The upshot of this story, and you'll be glad to know I have a point, is that 'Fairfax' strawberries are no longer available in commerce. The last nursery discontinued them a few years back. Why? Because 'Fairfax' doesn't bear as many berries as the newer varieties, and because, when ripe, they bruise more easily in shipping.

This is how I happen to know that, strawberrywise, we could be doing better than we are. One of the varieties I grow now, a variety called 'Sparkle', is a cross between 'Fairfax' and another strawberry called 'Aberdeen'. As I've said, these strawberries are pretty damn fine, but 'Sparkle' doesn't hold a patch on its parent. Have you noticed that, across the board, that's often the case?

Anyway, this business of varieties is relatively recent, starting around 1810 with some breeding, not a lot, in Europe. Until then, only the species were grown, species like alpine and Chili and *Fragaria virginiana,* the scarlet strawberry, as it was commonly known. These made small berries, like the ones you measured, except for the Chili Strawberry, which has mild-flavored fruits, larger in size. That's probably why it was so popular here, although most nineteenth-century writers dismissed *F. chiliensis* as being finicky to grow, not well adapted to North American conditions. You ordered it frequently, first from Bartram and later from M'Mahon. A few years ago it was immortalized on a T-shirt sold at Monticello, in the Garden Shop, and by mail.

'Hovey' was the first American introduction, in 1843, and although productive and big-fruited, it was hardly an immediate hit. According to Andrew S. Fuller, who wrote *The Illustrated Strawberry Culturist* several decades later, ". . . while a few cultivators may be said to have taken the hint, or avail themselves of this discovery, the larger majority continued to import varieties of the Chili Strawberry only to be sadly disappointed. . . ." Nonetheless, the concept of strawberry breeding made enough of an impact that by the time Peter Henderson drew up his ten-best list, in 1867, he had to pick from "a collection of fifty leading sorts."

A few more decades later, *only* the cultivated varieties were widely available, though most of them boasted *F. chiliensis* or *F. virginiana* in their lineage. Interestingly, these new and improved berries, initially so hard to catch on, were actually responsible for exploding the popularity of the fruit in general. Although a fairly old garden crop, strawberries were considered a bit esoteric, even in your day. Maybe because of that shipping problem again. Or maybe because being puny, people didn't want to be bothered with them.

If those were the obstacles, they no longer exist. First strawberries got bigger and bigger, then they got tough. I've already told you my 'Fairfax' story, so I won't dwell on the diminishing flavor. I will simply tell you that whatever flavor remains, it is one of America's favorites. Strawberries are everywhere, in jam, in ice cream, in pancakes, in yogurt. There is strawberry soda, strawberry cereal, strawberry bubblegum, and strawberry daiquiris. There are even, God help us, strawberry candles and soap.

As far as just strawberries go, Jimmy and I eat them mostly in season. Naturally, I don't shove them aside if I'm invited to dinner at other times of the year, but here at home, they are another crop, like asparagus before them, that we gorge ourselves on while they last, then wait until next year. Unlike asparagus, though, there are a few exceptions to this rule, and they are the packages of berries that actually make it out of the garden and into the freezer. One of them is brought out at Christmas, every year, and the berries are rolled up inside the crepes Jimmy makes for breakfast. A nice memento of summer.

I know I'm jumping ahead of myself by telling you this now. I know it's only the second of May. The first asparagus came to table only just today, the strawberries are still weeks away. But the one follows the other in such seamless succession, it's impossible to talk about the one without the other coming to mind. So while we feast on our roasted asparagus, napped with a perfectly poached egg, one antenna will be up and waving in anticipation of the strawberries. Because guess what? The 'Fairfax' are coming. They may be gone from commerce, but you don't think I'd let something that good disappear from the garden, do you? I'm not taking any bets on their coming to table, however. My guess is they will all be eaten, squatting barefoot, in the bed.

Please accept the assurance
of my great esteem and respect,

L. Simon

Dear Mr. Jefferson

It's been quite a while since I last sat down to write. The reason isn't lack of gardening news to report. It's actually the opposite. Too much news. Too much to do, at any rate. I don't know how newsworthy it is.

The oversized month between the fifteenth of May and the twentieth of June is the most frantic and exhausting of the garden year. In that month, at least seventy-five percent of the garden gets planted. And when I say garden now, I mean not only the kitchen garden, with its twenty-seven beds, but every ornamental border, window box, clay pot, and washtub as well. It's a lot of work, and I come into the house at twilight, sunburned, mosquito-bitten, grubby, and beat. It feels terrific.

Part of this pressure is due to the Nantucket spring, which I have disparaged with regularity and vigor, as I'm sure you've noted. It is not reliably frost-free until Memorial Day, at the soonest, before which time, and for two weeks after, it can be rainy, foggy, raw, sodden, or mercilessly windy, for days, without letup. Or all of them at once. Or, on rare, divine occasions, none of the above. The point is, though, I can't count on it. So I hold off planting as long as I can, until suddenly everything needs to go into the ground *now*. The cold frames are jammed full, as are the shanty and the nursery. The seedlings, no longer baby plants but robust adolescents, are spilling out of their six-packs, growing lankier while I watch, as teenagers are wont to do.

I did, however, say that seventy-five percent of the garden

was planted during this marathon month, which means that twenty-five percent of it goes in before or after the big push. A portion of this percentage is planted in summer, when I set out or sow the vegetables we harvest all fall and, some of them, all winter. Another portion gets planted between now and the first of July. All right, maybe by the tenth. I'm running out of steam. These are mostly the stragglers, the leftovers, the last scraps of flowers. Gawky, pinched-looking plants that, not so very long ago, were lovingly sown in the nursery, then tranquilly transplanted in the shanty. Incapable of tossing them on the compost heap after so much time spent together, I find unoccupied corners or empty terra-cotta pots, where, almost always, they perk up and flourish. Or at least enjoy a certain quality of life before they perish with the first frost, as they were meant to.

The symbolic final act of planting is to fill the cold frames with cosmos, and cleome, and zinnias, not scrawny leftovers but seedlings grown and waiting specifically for that purpose. Like so many other symbolic acts, though, this one is more symbol than final since the cold frames actually get planted as they are vacated, usually well before the last straggler finds a home. That's because, weary and increasingly anxious to get this thing over with, I cram the remnants of flats into the auxiliary cold frame behind the shanty, or leave six-packs of sorry-looking plants strewn about the lawn, unprotected overnight, on the off chance that browsing deer will make a midnight snack of them, relieving me of responsibility, if not necessarily of guilt. But why should the deer eat the flowers I have all but ceased to care about, when they could instead eat the ones that enchant me, the ones just beginning to bloom, prettily, in the borders?

That conundrum aside, I think I have accounted for a percentage of the unplanted percentage, but don't ask me at this moment to figure out how much. All I know is, if it wasn't a leftover, and it wasn't a fall crop, it got planted before all the madness started, back when I still nurtured the illusion that I had things under control. Since I never plant anything in April, or seldom, even, until after the asparagus comes to table, that last portion, or first one, more correctly, must have been planted between the fourth or fifth of May and the ides of the month. I don't know that I deliberately set this schedule. More likely the weather did it for me.

I have long since given up imagining that I have to plant my peas by St. Patrick's Day or my potatoes by Easter, or any of those other deadlines imposed on mainland gardeners. I've tried planting peas early. I might as well put the seeds under my pillow at night for the pea fairy to sprinkle with grow dust while I dream. Peas may like cool weather, even to the extent of withstanding a late frost, but they have no stomach for endless cold, gray days and cold, soggy soil. In protest of such treatment, they sprout poorly or rot in the ground. Or simply sit there, refusing to budge. It is far better, I've learned, to wait until the first decent day of May, when we both enjoy the experience more, and when the chances for ultimate success are dramatically greater.

As for the potatoes, it doesn't matter what day I pick, because that day invariably is utterly miserable. Even if sunshine and tropical temperatures are predicted, even if, when I start, the sky is blue and the air is gentle, without fail, before I'm done planting, it turns gray and bleak, and cold, fat raindrops fall, beating against my eyelids and cheeks, numbing my hands, chilling my bones. This, too, is tradition.

Planting potatoes is not something I do by myself. Jimmy and I do it together, or at least in tandem. First I cut the seed potatoes into pieces containing two or more eyes, leaving all tubers "the size of a hen's egg" whole, as per the instructions in the Ronniger's catalog. Sometimes I do this the night before, so the cuts can scab over. Sometimes it doesn't get done until the morning of. Either way, they make a handsome sight, a lovely pattern, all those potato pieces in green plastic trays, arranged on the living room floor, each tray identified with a marker made from a shard of wooden shingle.

Next, Jimmy digs the trenches, usually six of them in a bed, carefully piling the excavated soil in mountains alongside the valleys he's creating. Then I crawl backward down each trench, laying potato pieces before me, anchoring each one in place with a handful of dirt. By the second row, approximately, if the day has been at all promising, the sky begins to blacken and the temperature plummets. By row four, the raindrops start, splattering me in the face and soaking my sweater, turning the handfuls of dirt into handfuls of mud.

Jimmy stands ready to rake the mountaintops into the valleys of potatoes, covering the pieces, for now, about four inches deep. Except, that is, for the two rows in the middle, which, being out of reach from the path, I have to heap up as I sidle backward. As soon as the last muddy clod hits its trench, we grab up our tools and beat it for the house, reminding ourselves that our reward for this wretched day's work will come not in Heaven but in July, when the first 'Nosebag' fingerlings come to table, melting in our mouths.

We have another planting act, Jimmy and I, this one also smooth and practiced, this one also performed around the middle of May. In this act, we nestle new strawberry crowns in the earth, Jimmy prying apart the soil, the width of his shovel while I fan out the roots and slip the crown into the slit. Down the rows we go, dreaming, this time, about the sun-warmed berries sliding down our throats.

Let me say a word here about this business of rows. I'm a firm believer in them, in their separate beds, despite the current trend toward clusters and bunches. In the ornamental borders, I plant in spills and sweeps, but when it comes to vegetables, I find geometry appealing. This goes back, I guess, to the argument about what is beauty and whose eyes are beholding it. To trot out another axiom, when my eyes are involved, form follows function. Vegetables are as practical as it comes. That's part of their beauty. Another part, in the garden, is their ease of picking. I like the look that waves me over and says, "Yo. I'm ripe and delicious. Take me home for dinner." Not the look that sniffs, "I'm a still life. Admire me, but don't mess up the effect."

I extend this criterion to the cutting beds, where flowers march down rows like a high school band in a Fourth of July parade. These flowers were meant for bouquets, their artistic destinies are in vases. It just so happens that the beds are vivid and beautiful, but this is a bonus, not the main purpose. The main purpose is for me to be able to cut as many flowers as are in perfection of bloom, the same way I pick every vegetable that's ripe and begging to be eaten. As long as they are in rows, same as the vegetables, I can cut the flowers freely and make my arrangements in the house. Once I start composing them in beds, however, I'm again loath to disturb the still life, the same as with the vegetables.

Every task in the garden seems to have its own special tools, and row making is no exception to this rule, the implements for this job being stakes, string, tape measure, and mallet, stacked in a crate meant to hold one legal bushel of Nantucket bay scallops. Dede always rolled her eyes when she saw the kit coming out, but she graciously acceded, seldom making more than one wisecrack, two at the most. She got to the point where she anticipated the need herself and went to get the kit, without even waiting for a response to her rhetorically asked, "I don't suppose you want to eyeball it?" Because, no, I rarely want to eyeball it. My eyeballs aren't that good.

The truth of the matter is, though, Dede was usually not around at row-making time. When you get right down to it, Jimmy usually isn't, either. Making rows and planting the garden is, for the most part, something I do alone, with only Roger and Homer, Jack and Olive as witnesses. I love planting, just as I love sowing the seeds and transplanting the seedlings. It's peaceful and satisfying, despite the racket in the cold frames from plants demanding to go in the ground.

It's also the last time I handle them, these babies of mine. The dear little seedlings I raised from specks of matter, coddling them and encouraging them, are finally on their own. A lot of things can happen as the summer progresses—drought, fog, fungus, bugs, or maybe even ideal conditions. Whatever is going to happen, it will reveal itself when it's ready. For now, though, one last time, I am charged with hope and expectation.

So I sit in my red wagon, calculating the rows in my notebook before laying out the tape, driving in the stakes, and stretching the twine from one to another. The plants go in next, along the guitar-string taut line, unless it's peas, beans, root crops, or greens, in which case I sow seeds, lettuce excluded. At the end of the day, the bed is neatly striped, either with slight furrows, beneath which are seeds, or with small mounds of leaves, those boisterous seedlings suddenly looking mighty subdued in the big world of the garden.

I like to believe that all this talk of stakes and strings is falling on sympathetic ears. Ellen remembers you going out to your gardens with Wormley, "measuring-line" in hand, surely a sign that some row making went on at Monticello, too. Which, we ought to reassure the uninitiated, in no way means the end result looks rigid and restrained. The rows are made up of plants, after all, and what plant has any idea it's supposed to toe a line? Or, for that matter, that it's supposed to grow up in regimental symmetry? Plants climb, they sprawl, they lean, they meld. Even the straightforward onions manage to look rakish in their multiple rows. By the middle of July, it would take a detective to know a stake and string had ever been present.

I'll tell you one bed where I get a little bit fancy. It's the bed, or the edge of the bed, where I plant the *Capsicum annuum,* or peppers, for short. The first peppers I ever grew, back in the beginning, produced gnarled, nasty fruits, and not too many of them. Disgusted, I gave up on peppers for a number of years. Then, in my search for the tear-producing *piment* that Susan and I ate on *poisson grillé* when we lived in the Seychelles, I came across 'Thai Hot', darling, petite plants with peppers that will knock your socks off. I started growing those. Then more of them, because Chin, my friend from Thailand, who eats them by the handful, is always calling me up in a hot-pepper emergency, needing a refill.

Soon enough I had added 'Long Red Slim' cayenne peppers to the repertoire, because they make fantastic scarlet curlicues on the bush, and when dried and chopped into flakes, they really jazz up a pizza. Pizza, by the way, is a classic example of late-twentieth-century cuisine, combining the ease of a snack food with the substance of supper.

Buoyed by the hot-pepper success, I tried yellow 'Sunbright' bells next, more because the packet of seeds came free with an order than because of any deliberate decision, but the result was so wonderfully flavorful, I was off and running. I now grow six or eight varieties, between hot and sweet, and instead of setting the plants out in rows, I make a pepper composition, usually on the edge of the sweet-potato bed.

Really, though, even if I wanted to, I don't have time to get creative with every bed in the garden. It's more important to get them planted. Twenty-seven beds are a lot to do, but you know that. You had twenty-seven beds on your vegetable terrace, too.

Besides, just because the vegetables get planted in rows doesn't mean the garden ends up looking like industrial agriculture. Almost every row, or every series of rows, is planted in a different vegetable, creating a patchwork pattern of different textures, and different heights, and, to a lesser extent, different colors, a look that is underscored by rows that run in different directions. Then, too, some of the rows have additional decoration. Some of them have borders of flowers, some of the borders are hedges, some of the hedges don't go down the sides but slice through the middle. There are the structures Jimmy builds with saplings he cuts in the woods, a bean tepee rising amongst the broccoli, or a trellis with cucumbers climbing up the sides and cup-and-saucer vines and sweet peas climbing up the ends. Modestly speaking, it looks pretty good.

While on the subject of decoration, let me take a moment to mention the terra-cotta pots and the window boxes I cram full of flowers every year. I don't know how much gardening of this sort you did, if any at all. Your only use for earthen pots, as you called them, seems to have been for covering the sea kale, for which purpose you ordered "½ hundred" from a potter near Richmond in 1821. Some of your maps do show strategically placed urns, but it is an Olympic leap from there to imagine window boxes on the Palladian face of your home.

To be honest, window boxes aren't quite the thing for my house, either, though it is nowhere nearly as grand, or as formal, as yours. The chickens and the ducks, however, are adamant about having them under the two windows of their house, claiming that the planters are the only bit of garden going on behind the fence that keeps them from rummaging through mine. (Although the ducks have figured out, only last month, how to slip through that fence and go for a stroll across the lawn and a dip in the stream.) The poultry further insists that the floral displays be changed with the seasons, and, not wanting an insurrection on my hands, I do its bidding.

First thing in the spring are some miniature daffodils, their bright yellow as welcome a sight against the gray shingles as it is on the hillside down to the stream. When the daffodils wane, they are replaced by the pansies that have survived the winter in the garden, plants that were going to be evicted anyway, to make room for new tenants. The pansies seem as thrilled with this arrangement as the chickens, and respond with a riotous burst of blossoms not usually associated with these modest biennials.

The pansy show is finished in June, at which time I fill the window boxes with bold-colored annuals that will bloom until frost. At that point, if I'm feeling benevolent, I'll buy a few chrysanthemums at Bartlett's and jam them, pots and all, into the boxes to tide the girls over until Dede begins selling her Christmas trees at Moor's End Farm, the day after Thanksgiving. That's when I beg some of the branches she trims away, which, when stuck into the dirt, stay surprisingly fresh, not browning up until the daffodils start to emerge. I'm convinced the chickens and ducks appreciate my efforts and reward me by laying those epicurean eggs. At least that's what I tell people who rave about their flavor, that the window boxes are responsible for the fine food experience.

There is no extra reward, only garden-variety pleasure, for the other containers I fill with flowers, usually in June. For the terra-cotta pots shouldering their way up every porch step until it is nearly impossible to pass, for the tubs and basins framing the barn doors of the garage and crowding off the small dock of the shanty. You might think that with a huge and colorful kitchen garden just across the yard, and with overflowing borders so close to the house they climb up its shingles and over its rails, that all this might be excessive. Let me amend that. Other people might think so, but I doubt that you would.

I have half a hundred earthen pots myself. Or maybe twice that many. I don't know. I've given up counting. I just keep filling. I didn't acquire them all at one go, but accumulated them gradually over the years, replacing each one that froze and flaked away, or was backed over by a truck, with several or three others. Lest you think me incurably profligate, let me assure you that these pots, with only a few exceptions, are neither hand-thrown in simple English and American styles nor hand-coiled into the fabulously ornate creations Italian potters have been making since time out of mind.

At a certain point, toward the end of the last century, modern manufacturing technology overtook garden pots and they began to be mass-produced for tiny fractions of what individually crafted ones cost. Suddenly pots of geraniums and ivy appeared on every porch in America. In this century, especially with the gardening Renaissance of recent years, container gardening has come into its own. This practice, just as it sounds, means making a whole garden exclusively in pots.

There is a distinct difference between creating a garden in containers and just sticking a few annuals in pots, as I do, for summer display. I don't know too much about this branch of horticulture, though I'm learning some by osmosis, because my sister keeps a truly lovely container garden in New York. Susan has what amounts to a small miracle in Manhattan: a terrace. A large, private space outside her doors. As private, that is, as any outdoor space can be in a city that is home to a million more citizens in its five boroughs than inhabited the entire United States on the last day of your residence in 1826. Apart from the population issue, it is an exceedingly pleasant experience to dine on Susan's terrace amid the pots of shrubs, flowers, and honeysuckle. (And on Susan's food.) She even has a fig tree, something I wouldn't dare try.

It sometimes seems, during June, that figs are the only thing I don't grow. Day after day, I fill my red wagon, repeatedly, with flats of plants, which I wheel out to the garden, or to the borders, where I commit them to earth. Yet at day's end, the cold frames are still brimming over, the beds are filled up, and I'm running out of pots. It is in the next few weeks, actually, in the post-prime planting period, that my collection of pots sees its most significant annual increase.

I can't tell you how many fish totes of potting soil Jimmy

has churned up in the cement mixer he got when The Old Spouter potter retired from making soup bowls with whales on them and moved to Florida. One-third garden soil, one-third old manure, and one-third sand, this formula hasn't failed me, yet. Though *I* have been known to fail before *it* is finished.

It's hard to know precisely when the line is crossed between filling enough pots or planting enough decorative hedges to create the effect I want, and planting automatically, using up every last seedling. There is always a notation on my gardening calendar, always in capital letters and surrounded by exclamation points, sometimes even stars, depending on my level of relief, !!!GARDEN DONE!!! But is that day really when it's done? Or, here's another possibility, is that day still in the future?

Setting aside the philosophical argument that no garden is ever done, no more than a life is done until the last breath is drawn, there will still be plenty to do of an entirely untheoretical nature. There will still be the perennials and biennials to take care of, the ones I started this year from seed and have been largely ignoring for weeks. They'll need to get transplanted from their six-packs into the one-gallon pots in which they'll summer, sitting atop an old carpenter's bench in the sunshine behind the shanty, before being transplanted again, in September, into their permanent garden homes. More to come, too, as some vegetables finish and are replaced by others, with starts of lettuce and cilantro continuing at several-week intervals, and arugula getting sown directly in the garden approximately once a month. What the calendar note more appropriately should say is Round One Is Done, but there is just a little square for every day, and I have to save room in it for the stars and exclamation points.

Nevertheless, it will be a thrilling moment when that milestone is passed, whatever it is. It is a great production, this garden, an enormous orchestration, a theatrical event almost, in which the planting is akin to directing the players and painting the sets. When every potato is in place, every pole bean trained to its trellis, every nierembergia packed into its pot, then the curtain lifts and the show begins. With a little luck and a lot of sunshine, the applause will be thunderous.

Please accept the assurance
of my great esteem and respect,

L. Simon

Dear Mr. Jefferson

My annual brush with container gardening is inspired, as I said, less by true dedication to this horticultural specialty than by my desire to keep decorating after the ornamental borders are full. Excepting, of course, the tubs of mints that sit in the herb bed and between the eggplant. In this instance, the tubs serve to prevent the mint roots from worming their way through the entire garden, and their placement amongst the eggplant serves to prevent flea beetles from chewing so many pinholes in the leaves that I can use them for tea strainers. Flea beetles, according to gardening lore, find mint extremely disagreeable.

Whatever the case with flea beetles and containers, I have recently discovered a gardening niche that more fully captures my interest. This one, less common than its cousin, doesn't have a quick, handy catchphrase it goes by, so I call it, rather unceremoniously, Planting Flowers for the Bees. Properly speaking, my endeavor is only a fragment of the niche as a whole, making it, I suppose, a mere subsection of the avocation ancillary to my fascination with gardening overall. Maybe I'd better explain.

To satisfy even one colony of bees with any one species of flower, it's necessary to plant an eighth of an acre of them, or thereabouts, enough nectar, in other words, for roughly sixty thousand suppers. To put it in a more manageable perspective, just one worker foraging food for the bees waiting back at the hive will sip nectar from fifty to a hundred blossoms before heading, at twelve miles an hour, for home.

Since Jimmy has four colonies and I plant only a few dozen of each appetizing flower, my efforts are more on the order of hors d'oeuvres at a cocktail party than a seven-course, sit-down dinner. Here I am imagining that I'm laying out an irresistibly tempting spread, but the bees are probably disgusted, thinking me a tease. "If she were really serious about Planting Flowers for the Bees," the buzz inside the hive undoubtedly goes, "she'd plant whole meadows of sweet clover and forget-me-nots and echinacea and lavender." Would that I had a meadow at my disposal. It would be my pleasure to make a banquet fit for a queen. And her subjects.

You seem to be silent on the subject of bees, and of honey as well. No mention of them in the Garden Book, not even a casual reference in any of your letters. From this silence I can only infer that either you didn't have a sweet tooth or that bees, at Monticello, were taken for granted, not kept. Considering your persistent attempts to grow sugar maples in order to reap their syrupy dividend, I'd have to say that the former supposition, your lack of a sweet tooth, doesn't hold water.

It is conceivable, however, that the latter one does, especially when I put the discussion in its context, remembering the date, and the state of beekeeping, at the time that you gardened. *Apis mellifera,* our own dear honeybees, aren't native Americans, although they were very early colonists. History tells it that they crossed the Atlantic shortly after the Pilgrims did, and were in residence up and down the entire eastern seaboard within a decade or so, certainly by the 1640s. Since bees will be bees, given to swarming from the day they evolved, soon enough the immigrants split off from their mother hives and found their own hollow trees, establishing a population that was, if not indigenous, at least undomesticated. In this manner, honeybees moved west faster than human settlers, earning the appellation "white man's flies" from those Americans who were more genuinely Native.

I'm not exactly sure what the bee census was during your tenure, but I do know that the art and science of beekeeping in those days was terribly inexact, ironic, really, since bees themselves are so fastidious and precise. People back then didn't *keep* bees so much as they *had* them, hit or miss. They went out to the woods, cut down a tree with bees in it, and plunked the log in their yard, unlike today when a package of them arrives in the mail. Harvesting the honey, furthermore, was a crude process, involving a lot of grief for all associated parties, though probably the bees fared the worst. Despite some late-eighteenth-century discoveries about the habits of bees, by a blind Swiss naturalist named François Huber, this essentially was the way beekeeping was done from the time of the ancient Egyptians until October 30, 1851.

It's rare, I think, for dramatic advance to occur so abruptly. Nonetheless, that was what happened to beekeeping when Lorenzo Lorraine Langstroth, a Philadelphia minister prone to nervous disorders, was walking home from his bee-yard late on that afternoon. "Seeing by intuition, as it were, the end from the beginning, I could scarcely refrain from shouting out my 'Eureka!' in the open streets," the reverend remembered years later.

What he realized, after years of pondering and trial, was

that bees want exactly three eighths of an inch of space for passageways inside their hives. Give them any less, and they will glue the space closed with propolis, a mortar they make from the resin in buds, sap, and bark. Give them any more, and they will fill it with comb. Either way, the hive becomes an impenetrable fortress, and getting the honey out is an unhappy battle.

The discovery of bee space led to Langstroth's invention of the movable frame hive, a square wooden box in which the wax comb hangs in wooden frames, like files in a cabinet. Each frame adheres, strictly, to the prescription for bee space, hanging three eighths of an inch from the ceiling, from the walls, from the floor, and three eighths of an inch from each other. With the creation of this hive, respectful of the bees even as it provides easy access to their honey, an industry, a science, and an art were simultaneously born. Even more fatefully, though, the stage was set for Jimmy, who came along one hundred and forty-three years after Langstroth's lightning bolt, and fell head over heels.

I have to confess that, fascinating as I find bees, I doubt I would keep them by myself. For one thing, a lot of the keeping takes place at a time when I don't have a minute to spare—in the spring, for instance, when I'm getting the garden started, or in the fall, when I'm harvesting it. For another thing, though, L. L. Langstroth's boxes are heavy! The ones Jimmy takes off, gleaming with honey to extract for our larder, weigh around fifty-five pounds each, every ounce of it sticky. The ones he leaves for the bees to sup on all winter are upwards of eighty pounds, hoisted from a standstill.

Jimmy is constantly wrestling with the boxes, stacking and unstacking them, lifting out each frame. He's checking for signs that the queen is alive and well, and that all the members of her court are doing the jobs that evolution assigned them. During the course of her six-week life, the worker bee graduates from one assignment to another, and this is the part of beekeeping that I find so intriguing.

How does the newborn bee, all fuzzy and fresh, know that the first job that awaits her is to clean up her room? She does it without hesitation, though, just as soon as she's eaten. She makes the cell she emerged from clean as a whistle. The queen inspects it with her antennae, preparatory to laying another egg, and if it doesn't pass muster, the young bee, presumably, gets a royal scolding. From chambermaid, she moves on to nurse-maid, feeding the brood in the uncapped cells. By day seven of her life, she is ready to tackle any housekeeping chore that needs doing, grooming and feeding the queen, for instance, or fanning her wings to regulate the temperature. At a certain age, usually day ten, she produces the wax that's needed to build cells, or to seal off the ones that hold either honey or larvae.

Scullery maid is another position these young bees assume, going down to the hive entrance to meet the incoming for-agers. In an archetypal example of feminine cooperation, the foragers transfer the nectar and pollen they've gathered to the house bees, who either store it in cells for future meals or distribute it directly to whichever of their colleagues is hungry. In meat-and-potatoes type terms, bees eat the pollen for its protein, while the nectar provides them with carbohydrates.

As the last step in their multitudinous careers, the worker bees fly out of the hive to gather these groceries. They stick the pollen into hairy "baskets" on the backs of their legs. The nectar goes into a special stomach, where enzymes start turning it, immediately, to honey. Always organized and efficient, these foragers don't waste time window-shopping but fly straight away to flowers that reconnaissance bees have told them about in their morning reports.

Although they are game to fly two, or even three, miles to find a meal, our lucky bees have plenty to eat much closer to home. I'm not speaking, yet, about the meager snacks I take such delight in providing but about the woods all around us, in which quantities of the bees' favorite foods grow. First to appear, when almost everything else is still dormant, are the red maples, making brilliant red flowers loaded with both pollen and nectar. The bees love it. It's just the boost they need. Walk under any *Acer rubrum* on a sunny spring day, including the Medusa-like maple forty feet off the corner of the garden, and you can hear the whole tree humming, the sound of bees at a feast.

Later on, the tupelos bloom. Black gum. *Nyssa sylvatica*, not the more replete species of tupelo that bloom farther south. Still, the flowers of these northern trees hold a soupçon of nectar each, which, when multiplied by the thousands of flowers on every tree and again by the scores of tupelos in the woods, makes a respectable repast. The menu changes again with the dogwoods, then again with the shadblow, and the blueberries, and then again when the sweet pepperbush blooms in August. Even more treats await the industrious foragers in the open field at the end of our driveway, where daisies and thistles and countless drifts of goldenrod flower in nourishing sequence. And if they're feeling energetic, on a bright day in June, they can make a beeline for the world's largest natural cranberry bog, only a mile and a half away.

Then there is the garden, even before I start adding to it. Just the regular stuff, the things I grow for us, the honeybees also enjoy. We seem to share an appreciation of many of the same flowers, like bachelor's buttons, Canterbury bells, and asters, although my interest is purely aesthetic, while the bees are thinking of food.

Our motives converge when it comes to the vine crops, however, especially cucumbers, but also the melons. While you already know how crazy Jimmy is about his cantaloupes, it may surprise you to learn the bees share his ardor. I find it an amusing congruity that bees and keeper have a craving in common, even if Jimmy's is the fruit and the bees' is the flower that precedes it. Actually, the relationship is more entwined still, because Jimmy wouldn't have his fruit if the bees didn't consider its flower a delectable morsel.

Bees, specifically honeybees, are vital to the pollination of all the cucurbit family, to which melons and cucumbers belong. Although it must be said that pumpkin and squash, which are also members of this family, are much further down on the honeybees' list. The flowers of pumpkins and squash open up at dawn, you see, and are already closing by nine, which is usually before the bees have gotten the scouting reports and have the day's agenda planned. I understand completely. I'm not a morning person, either.

This, however, is not what I wanted to tell you, because I've always planted a kitchen garden, and somehow, even before the advent of *Apis mellifera* in our lives, it always got pollinated. Wait. Let me correct that. The kitchen garden always got pollinated, excluding the orchard. The orchard is another story entirely. For years, we waited patiently while our fruit trees grew and made flowers, but though they looked reasonably healthy, all we ever harvested were three or four peaches and a handful of apples. The trouble was, we eventually figured out, fruit trees bloom too early in our reluctant spring to attract the attention of shivering insects, still half-hibernating.

It was precisely this problem that piqued Jimmy's interest in bees. Initially, he was thinking of the orchard, with not the slightest clue about the infatuation that would befall him. But even apart from this felicitous outcome, acquiring bees was pure inspiration. With the hives situated mere yards from the orchard, the bees can nip over at any spring moment when there's a break in the bleakness. The result is, of course, that as they grab a quick bite, they pick up grains of pollen from one blossom, which they carry to the next. The ultimate result, the happy ending to this story, is a hearty meal for the bees and, finally, abundant fruit for us. There's even a bonus. Honey. Lots of it. Bottles and jars full. Enough honey for the bees to eat all winter and enough honey for us. Enough honey for tea, enough honey for toast, enough honey to make barbecue sauce, enough to give away as gifts.

As far as the garden end of all this goes, I was already doing it. The orchard was there and so, annually, were the cucumbers, the campanula, the asters, the melons. Where the new fun begins is in growing plants I never have before. It comes from having a reason—no, make that a responsibility—to grow plants we neither eat nor ever thought of putting into vases. So when the seed orders get bigger and the space under the lights gets more squeezed, the gleeful excuse I can offer is that I'm doing it for the bees. This is an unassailable argument, absolutely irrefutable, and gardening aside, tell me, how often in life do we land on the right side of one of those?

Even better for me, though, gardening is not an aside but

the main issue, which is why I sent away for seeds, among others, of *Dipsacus sylvestris.* More commonly called teasel, this tall, bespiked herb looks almost prehistoric when it sways, ominously, in the winter wind. It has only one post-pterodactyl use that I know about, and, in an interesting small-world coincidence, I wrote about it in one of my novels, a novel that had as its background the nineteenth-century manufacture of woolen cloth. This industry, a monument to human toil and shrieking machinery, depended upon *Dipsacus,* a mere plant, for the finishing touches.

The seedpod of teasel is shaped like an egg but is covered with curved spines between which tiny lavender flowers bloom in early July. That's when the bees have a picnic, sticking to the pod like specimens pinned onto velvet, extracting a nectar that, purportedly, makes a nearly white honey. No one grows enough of it these days to verify that fact, but a hundred and more years ago, farmers, mostly in New York State, grew acres and acres of it. They waited until the flowers were done and the pods were dried to their primordial form, then cut down the stalks and shipped them to the wool mills, mostly in Massachusetts. There, the bristly pods were used to brush up the nap of the newly woven woolens, in some cases to shear it off flat, as with worsteds, in other cases just to card it.

Despite its moment in history, and my own roundabout connection to it, I don't think I'll be growing teasel again, at least not intentionally. For one thing, it's a biennial, which, of itself, is perfectly fine, but the first year it's barely a foot tall, and the second year it's over seven. That, too, would be acceptable, because, when tall, it makes such a dramatic show, unless a hurricane comes through, as Eduardo did, and seven feet of fierce prickles and spikes is no longer vertical but sprawled across the sorrel. My true objection, though, is teasel's ability to prolifically self-sow. I picked hundreds of teasel seedlings out of the herb bed this spring, and I have the feeling that come the millennium, I'll be picking them out still.

The herb bed is another thing that happened when I began Planting Flowers for the Bees. Not that I didn't already have a small one, but I made it more than twice bigger by joining it to the grass path and the empty bed adjacent. Since a surprising number of the flowers the bees seem to favor are herbs, making more space for them was absolutely essential.

In the course of cooking, I don't use many herbs. Several basils, including the sweet, purple Thai, and single-leaf Italian parsley are the mainstays, although I've lately developed an addiction to mint and chives chopped together. I am also fond of sage, especially when rotisserizing a chicken, and even more so of rosemary, though I grow that in terra-cotta pots so I can bring it inside for winter stews. Herbs with a distinctly summer flavor, to my taste, are cilantro and dill, which also self-sows, but the dill I encourage because the volunteers are always fuller than the ones I deliberately plant. Don't get me wrong, the bees love all of these herbs, including the thyme, which I forgot to mention, but except for the dill and a few of the chives, generally speaking, I try to keep them from flowering. Selfishly, I want them to make foliage, not flowers, for use in *our* dinner.

I can't remember who or what guided me in compiling my original bee-plant list. Maybe the exhortations in seed catalogs. "Bees and Butterflies love it!!" Or maybe just extrapolation. Bees like herbs, therefore . . . I somehow feel there had to have been a certain amount of scientific reasoning, but as I've said in

187

the past, my memory is unreliable, and this is a perfect example of one of its lapses. Whether advertising or entomology, though, the list got made and the seeds got sowed, and the punch line is that my Muse was off the mark.

I have since learned that there are bees and then there are bees, and among other distinguishing features between species is the length of the tongue. For the record, the tongue of *Apis mellifera* is not among the long ones. Flowers that secrete nectar at the bottom of deep tubes are, therefore, more coveted by bumblebees and hummingbirds than by our tireless workers. Into this deep-throat category falls, wouldn't you know it, *Dipsacus sylvestris,* the teasel that will be with me, I fear, forevermore.

Also in this category is an herb I have no intention of discarding, *Hyssopus officinalis,* commonly called hyssop. I suspect that hyssop found a home in my garden through one of those extrapolations I mentioned. Bees love anise hyssop, therefore they must love hyssop, too. Which is, like *Mirabilis,* another argument in favor of botanical names, because while it's true that bees love anise hyssop, anise hyssop is actually not a hyssop at all but *Agastache foeniculum,* and is only distantly related to *Hyssopus officinalis* through a very large family.

They are both handsome plants and both make blue flowers, but beyond that, the similarity ends, quite decisively. *Hyssopus officinalis* is comparatively short and makes a well-behaved hedge, from which shoot spires bright with small indigo flowers. Anise hyssop, on the other hand, grows taller than I am, though all the seed catalogs and herbals swear that it tops out at four feet. Its leaves are bigger and more textured than those of the hyssop from which it takes its name, elongated hearts with serrated edges, as compared with the smooth, narrow foliage of *H. officinalis,* though they definitely live up to the anise part, smelling strongly of licorice. Of the two hyssops, this is the one the honeybees really adore, flying touch-and-go's around its bottlebrush flowers for as many hours as there is light in the day. They will make a polite pass at the other hyssop, however, just to show good manners. The queen brought them up well.

They also dutifully investigate the clump of *Monarda* I've planted for them. I had *Monarda* in my ornamental borders years ago, but I failed to be swept away by its shaggy flowers, which, to my eye, bear the look of having had their stems stuck in a light socket. Or, I should say, of having had Benjamin Franklin's kite string wrapped around them at an inopportune moment. But the common name of *Monarda* is bee balm (are you beginning to get the drift?), so once we got bees I felt obligated to reinstate *Monarda* in the garden. How could I deny our bees a flower that, apparently, soothed them?

False advertising, as it turns out. The bees of the title are, once again, *Apis bombus,* cheerful, chubby bumblebees, who live underground, not the *Apis mellifera,* who have hives full of honey. That pesky tongue problem. As I write this, I realize that my own tongue is somewhat in my cheek, because it's hard to keep from smiling when I imagine a dozen or so kinds of *Apis* sticking their tongues out for measurement. The truth is, though, this isn't a matter for laughter so much as it is for awe.

The nectar a flower makes serves one purpose only, to attract the insect needed to carry its pollen from anther to stigma, thus ensuring the survival of its species. The shape of the flower, therefore, is designed to accommodate the insect appropriate to the task, whether honeybee or ant or night-flying moth. Although honeybees, with their hairy bodies to which pollen clings like lint on a sweater, are by far the pollinators of choice, some plants, like spinach, grasses, and corn, don't need any assistants to pollinate them but instead rely on the wind. Other plants, whose flowers are called "perfect," need neither insects nor wind but take care of the pollinating chores themselves. These plants, self-pollinated or pollinated by the wind, don't bother to produce nectar, tiny droplets of sugar and water, which is scented, incidentally, as a further lure for the insects they're recruiting.

It is this grand scheme that, for me, inspires awe. How did this vast, intricate, overlapping, all-encompassing plan fall into place? How were the micrometric dimensions decided? How was the bee tongue fitted to the flower? And if the majority of plants are pollinated by bees, honeybees at that, why aren't the majority of flowers identical, one to the other? In that same vein, why does each plant secrete differing amounts of sugar and odor, and how did these recipes for nectar get concocted? Why, for instance, does the pear flower produce a nectar so low in sugar, it has almost no appeal for the bees? Is this an oversight, a cosmic goof, or are we in the middle of an evolutionary process, halfway along in the pears' transition to self-pollination? Or, more fundamentally, is this the work of a master orchardist who prefers apples and plums?

I think I sense myself crossing a thin, delicate line here, so I'd better desist. The only other thing I will say on the subject of beekeeping is that it's a pity L. L. Langstroth didn't have his Eureka fifty years sooner. As much as I am loath to make any assumptions on your behalf, I've got to believe that post-Langstroth beekeeping would have appealed to you enormously.

It combines many of the elements you were known to enjoy—science, gardening, food, and, better yet, carefully recorded data. About this last area, I can speak with a shred of authority, it being another contribution I make to Eat Fire Spring Apiary, besides Planting Flowers for the Bees. Almost as soon as he started keeping bees, I bought Jimmy an elegantly bound journal with beautiful, heavy pages, though he largely ignores it, scribbling his notes on a National Fisherman's calendar instead. Undaunted, I then made a Honey Log and gave it to him for Christmas, and, success at last, he uses that tiny book for recording jars of honey bottled. One hundred and sixty-two pounds, last season, in one, two, four, and five-pound jars. Doesn't this sort of information sound like a natural for you?

It's no secret that you relished a good farming equation or puzzle, so much so you even set up computable problems, then carried them to conclusion. "[P]lanted 2400. cuttings of weeping willow," you noted in 1794. "[A] man plants 800. to 1000. a day . . . if 8. willows will yeild 1. cord at a lopping, & bear lopping every 3d. year, then 800. of these may be lopped every year, & yield 100. cords of wood." Two years earlier you had figured out that "20 bushels of peaches will make 75 galls. of mobby i.e. $\frac{5}{12}$ of it's bulk."

These are good exercises, if somewhat straightforward. Think now, though, about the satisfaction involved in calculating the fields of different honey plants times the number of beehives, not forgetting to factor in the evaporation of water from the nectar before it becomes honey. If the worker bee forages on clover, for instance, in bloom half a mile from the hive, how many round trips does she make in her two-odd weeks of field work, and how much nectar does she gather? How much clover honey, furthermore, does one hive produce? One more clue.

Our dedicated bee, who lives only to serve, leaves behind just one twelfth of a teaspoon of honey, the sweet legacy of her industry and loyalty. As you can see, the mathematical possibilities are wonderful to contemplate, but, more to the point, so is the marvel.

Please accept the assurance
of my great esteem and respect,

L. Simon

Dear Mr. Jefferson

". . . [W]hen I return to live at Monticello," you wrote a friend from the confines of the presidency in 1803, ". . . I believe I shall become a florist. The labours of the year, in that line, are repaid within the year. . . ." Exactly.

I know you were thinking that you didn't dare indulge yourself by growing trees, your horticultural passion, that at sixty years of age you were already breathing borrowed air. It was not an unreasonable assumption in an era when men rarely reached fifty, and you had no way of knowing that, with twenty-three years of gardening still ahead of you, there was plenty of time for an acorn to become a mighty oak. Somewhat mighty, anyway. Under the circumstances, however, the decision to grow flowers seems sound.

Nor do I think you regretted having made it, or even considered it a second-class substitute, a consolation prize, so to speak. Rather, you embraced it with your customary inquisitiveness and zeal, designing the Roundabout Walk, for starters, with ample borders on either side of it to ensure that you wouldn't have to "restrain the variety of flowers" that might tempt you in the course of your new pursuit.

Within certain parameters, naturally. "I have an extensive flower border," you explained to Bernard M'Mahon, "in which I am fond of placing *handsome* plants or *fragrant*. those of mere curiosity I do not aim at." Again, I heartily concur. Although I must confess I give your words, both these and the ones above, an interpretation that is, I'll bet, a shade different from what you meant. All the same, I don't think it dishonors your intention.

I did not have to be won over to the cultivation of flowers. Quite the opposite of you, I prefer it to growing trees. Perhaps I am, unconsciously, already concerned about my mortality, always a chancy thing, no matter that longevity has extended by several decades since your day. More likely, though, I find flowers to be their own reward, their spectacular colors and exquisite shapes reason enough not only to plant them but to plant them with abandon.

Now here comes the part where I skew your meaning, where I use your eloquently expressed thoughts to legitimize my own. The flowers I am referring to are annuals. Did you read that right? Annuals. Flowers that spring from a seed, bloom, and die, all in one season, flowers whose labors "are repaid within the year." Furthermore, the annuals I favor are the classic ones, a vibrant spectrum of flowers that are "*handsome*" or "*fragrant.*" Not flowers that are exotic or obscure for obscurity's sake. Not those of "mere curiosity." This is a pretty radical admission, I realize.

You are probably unaware of how astounding it is. You may even be baffled by why I feel the need to justify such a statement, why I take cover under the authority of your opinions the way I once took cover under the portico at Monticello when it showered. I'll tell you why. Because annuals, for the past hundred or so years, have had an uneasy hold on horticultural respect. There has been a love/hate relationship between annuals and the arbiters of gardening taste. The beauty and verve these flowers bring to the garden have been grudgingly acknowledged, but still no one wants to come out, forcefully, on their side. A late-nineteenth-century seedsman said that annuals were "pre-eminently the flowers of the people." No one knows better than you what a hard position that is for aristocrats, royal or horticultural, to defend.

It wasn't always thus. The beleaguered annual is the victim of two antithetical gardening vogues, both of them born in England and washed up on our shores. The first was the phenomenon known as carpet bedding, beloved by Victorians in the middle of the nineteenth century. To achieve this aesthetic ideal, gardeners planted masses of annuals (or tulips, do you remember me telling you?), making ribbons of color, creating elaborate designs that indeed resembled the carpets the English still adore. In an effort to focus only on the positive, I will confine myself to saying that as a result of this craze, for the first time, great attention was paid to developing garden-worthy annuals and to breeding them in brilliant hues.

Although carpet bedding exists to this day, both in modified form and in the extreme state in which hapless flowers spell out words of welcome or advertisement on corporate lawns, this gardening epidemic pretty much ran its course. Or perhaps it would be more apt to say that it ran headlong into the second phenomenon, in the form of William Robinson, a gardener and writer whose life spanned nearly a century, from 1838 to 1935, and whose categorical opinions occasionally tilted toward the curmudgeonly.

William Robinson had little patience for either carpet bedding or its accomplice, topiary, which he felt was equivalent to "the cramming of Chinese feet into impossible shoes." But rather than just complaining, he proposed, and vigorously promoted, a solution. He called it "The Wild Garden," which, he assured his readers, has "nothing to do with the old idea of 'Wilderness.'" What he envisioned instead was "naturalizing many beautiful plants of many regions of the earth in our fields, woods and copses, outer parts of pleasure grounds, and in neglected places in almost every kind of garden." In other words, he was after a spontaneous look, a concept that seemed shocking when he set it forth but one that came to be accepted by the turn of our century and that has remained the guiding light of gardening for its entire length.

Although I certainly don't wish to turn back the clock on this garden style, I mourn the loss of esteem the annual suffered, by association, when carpet bedding fell, precipitously, from grace. Annuals became the scapegoat, I feel, going from much admired carpet to the sweepings underneath, faster than you could say William Robinson. How much easier to deprecate a plant that has no power of speech than to admit that Men displayed appalling arrogance in assuming that the dopey designs they were scrolling in lawns with ribbons of annuals were more desirable than the individual flowers themselves.

Oh sure, writers at the time of transition paid them compliments, albeit somewhat condescending in tone, but annuals never really recovered their former status. It doesn't help matters that the surviving examples of carpet bedding have shifted in location from swanky estates to the meridian strips of parking lots and the "green spaces" at shopping malls and amusement parks. Nor does it help that every supermarket and garden center, every spring, sells flats of annuals. Billions of thirsty-looking impatiens and marigolds and petunias, enduring unspeakable indignities as they wait, longingly, for a tiny scrap of ground, some place, any place, where they can flaunt their flowers, set their seeds, and die, fulfilled. Poor annuals. They have no cachet.

Which is why they all do so well in my garden, I'm convinced. They are grateful for the venue and for the sincere welcome they receive, not to mention the abundance of manure, and someone to pull the weeds that strangle their roots. Ah, bliss. In my garden, annuals are queens.

Not that I mean to effect an air of reverse snobbery, rejecting the infinitely more prestigious perennials that garden "designers" seem to prefer. I love perennials. The sight of six-foot-tall delphiniums and foxgloves makes me swoon, and a stand of lupines paralyzes me with pleasure. I have never, yet, encountered a campanula I didn't fall for instantly, inviting three species home on a permanent basis and welcoming others for guest appearances. And peonies. Oh my.

In 1923 Mrs. Alice Harding wrote of their "inescapable lure." A lure that is, for me, no less inescapable today. I am drawn, as fatally as a sailor to a Siren, by the clutter of their satiny petals in shades of cherub-dust pink, snow-white, and vermilion-rose, and, almost more, by their fragrance, for which mere adjectives are an insult. I even find the inevitable procession of ants marching across the open blossoms irresistible.

But wait. I was talking about annuals. See how easy it is to stray? I could take off on this perennial tack and talk about the erigeron and the maple-leaf anemone and the great blue lobelia, which I grew from seeds I bought at Monticello. It is a knockout at the back of the border, mingled with the French mallow, also from Monticello, and not quite perennial this far north. I'm not going to, though, because the front of the border is equally as lovely, and it is all annuals, with the exceptions of a few flowering shrubs, some purple irises that I searched the earth to find, an impressive birdbath scooped out of a wedge of pink New Hampshire granite, and a scattering of perennials, mostly over at the edges. It's the annuals, though, that steal the show.

By the Fourth of July they have completely filled the beds, obliterating every trace of underlying soil with their foliage and flowers, and a few weeks later they are overflowing them, obliterating now the Belgian block edging and creeping into the paths. Hundreds upon hundreds of pure white, daisy-dot 'Star White' zinnias; scores of thin, wiry sprays crowded with the tiny, violet-blue florets of 'Imagination' verbena. Springing up in their midst are the simple pink faces of 'Rose Pinwheel' zinnias, as well as two species of heliotrope, two blue salvias, and both the tall 'Blue Horizon' ageratum and the delightful stubby 'Royal Hawaii', which grows, like Victorian nosegays, between the pink granite birdbath and the Belgian block path. I had that path made, a little while back, after years of pleading, in vain, with the birds at the feeders to stop spitting out their empty seed hulls, making an unholy mess of the grass path the Belgian block replaced.

It is onto this same path that one clump of *Mirabilis longiflora* spills, opening up its ethereal white trumpets at twilight to perfume the evening air. Also along this path, and the scallop-shell one leading from the driveway to the porch, sit those terra-cotta pots I told you about, stuffed with double peony-flowered petunias, or dwarf 'Sonata' cosmos, or 'Mammoth' verbena, or surprise mixes of *Phlox drummondii,* all of them beautiful, some of them stunning.

All of these, and a fair number of others, are annuals. At least they are in my zone. Most of them are in bloom from the time they get going in early summer until frost strikes them dead, which, in a good year, might not be until the end of October. I'm talking about true bloom, now, about a continual profusion of flowers, not about the euphemistically called "repeat bloom" that certain perennials offer up. In my experience, repeat bloom means a couple of stunted versions of the original flower, coming several months after the first flush is over and done. All too often, these weaklings appear on plants that are still ragged-looking from having been cut back, making me wish they hadn't bothered to bloom, drawing my eye to them, and rousing pity for their reduced straits.

This bloom situation, I think, is at the heart of the argument in annuals' favor. Not that they can't stand on their own merits. They most assuredly can and they do. But the fact that the most glorious perennials are gone by the end of June, or July at the latest, means that I can only cast them a quick, admiring glance before I kneel, eyes to the earth, planting tomatoes, and potatoes, and seven kinds of beans, etc., etc. With rare exceptions, they aren't around in summer, or in September, the most magnificent month of the Nantucket calendar, when Roger, Jack, and I make leisurely, tea-time garden patrols, Olive and Homer ranging far out in front. Annuals, however, are still going strong.

They are there every morning when I take my shower, outside, the small, scarlet brushes of tassel flower tapping on my shin, the sky blue bells of *Nolana* nudging my toes. They are there when I sit in an Adirondack chair at the end of the path to dry in the sun, an abundance of flowers, an opulence, their stems dipping and swaying as honeybees and butterflies and hummingbirds alight. The sweet, heady fragrances are usually more apparent after sunset, but midmorning, in the sunshine, slight hints, a certain scent, drifts in the breeze. They are there, the annuals, and they are in color.

That part about the color is important. Vitally important. You have to understand that there are long periods of gray on Nantucket. I mean really gray. Gray sky, gray ocean, gray-shingled houses, gray branches on gray, leafless trees. Nantucket is, after all, The Gray Lady at Sea. No question, the intensity of gray sets a deep, brooding mood, one that dramatically heightens the solitude I honestly do enjoy. But after three or so months, enough is enough. The trouble is, it doesn't seem to be enough for Nantucket, and there are another three or so months until the daffodils bring the first real relief. Unless you count the cardinals that drop by the bird feeder all winter, and you'd better believe that I do.

Those six months of gray are why I need to saturate myself with color every summer. Why I keep planting annuals long after I've run out of space in the borders, stopping only when every terra-cotta pot I own is filled, or when the last gaunt China aster or *Salvia horminum* finds a home, whichever comes first. With annuals, I can load up on color, I can store away for winter the sensuous shades of long-blooming flowers, not unlike the honeybees, who are storing away their nectar. From the perfumed purple velvet of the low-growing heliotrope, to the five-foot-tall hedge of tithonia, whose brilliant egg-yolk orange flowers look as if they were carved out of soap, the colors of annuals get me through the gray.

Oh, I know. I've read the magazines and the picture books.

It's possible to achieve colorful results with perennials, too. All I have to do is overplant the early bloomers, and transplant in the later ones, and choose plants that bloom in staggered shifts throughout the season. First of all, this means a lot of fiddling with the borders at a time when I feel I've earned the right to be sitting on the porch with a glass of iced tea, and second, it's still not the summer extravaganza that annuals make. Third, though, the perennial route usually involves at least some santolina, which not only has yellow flowers, it has silver foliage. I know it's unimaginative of me, but I like my leaves green. Silver is too reminiscent of gray.

I am beginning to detect a defensive tone to my words, an attitude I intend to reverse forthwith. I don't plant annuals for what they are not but for what they are. I like this group of flowers. I have dear friends among them and look forward to them every year, first to raise them from seed in the nursery, and then to revel in their garden glory. "the labours of the year . . . repaid within the year. . . ."

Which leads me to make a rather uncharacteristic remark. Where annuals are concerned, I don't feel tremendous loyalty to history. While I'm always pleased to discover that an annual I like has ties to the past, the French mallow from Monticello being as perfect an example as exists, more usually I get so charmed by a flower, I only have eyes for its beauty. There are no 'Ravensworth' pea or 'Tennis Ball' lettuce yearnings attached to this branch of gardening. Where annuals are concerned, loveliness takes precedence over lineage.

It is almost impossible, for instance, for me to imagine my cutting bed without a row of 'State Fair' zinnias along the back edge, no matter that 'State Fair' was introduced in 1956, which hardly makes it historic, although it does have the distinction of being the first tetraploid bred. I have been known to think that these are my favorite flowers, that they surpass all others in those elusive standards that quantify superiority.

I love the boldness of these four-foot zinnias, the simplicity of their form, the clearness of their colors, their fundamental flowerness, as pure as a child's drawing. I love the tiny petals that sprout from their cushiony center disk, and the almost comical stamens that ring it, resembling the miniature antennae of friendly aliens or fantasy bugs. I love their coarse green leaves, strong and sturdy, but looking slightly slept in, and feeling like a two-day beard. This moment of inviolate infatuation always passes, of course, as soon as my adulterous gaze fastens on 'State Fair's nearest neighbor, but that's not to say it doesn't reoccur constantly.

At various times, and to varying degrees, I have fallen madly for various annuals for a variety of reasons. The freckles on the lower lip of 'Foxy' foxgloves' downturned bells, to cite one case, are so cunning they make me want to cluck them under the chin. The texture of *Scabiosa* just before its button of pinhead buds opens up is like that of a Renaissance tapestry or closely shorn silk velvet. And how about pansies? Strictly speaking, I know they are biennials, but they are always so eager to bloom, bursting into flowers bigger than they are even before they move out of their six-packs and into the garden, that I think of them as annuals, and paragons, at that. I would have to have the heart of Attila the Hun to resist their endearing faces, frowning up at me like myopic pandas.

There's hardly one annual, in fact, that I haven't loved above all others, if only for a moment, excluding, of course, the omnipresent impatiens. But lavatera, whose long, elegant buds unswirl so dramatically, reveals satiny pink cups that are breath-taking next to the blazingly blue fuzz of 'Blue Boy' bachelor's buttons. The slightly beserk loops that the stems of *suworowii* statice make elicit a feeling that's more amusement than passion. Still, there's no denying my fondness for its bright pipe-cleaner spikes.

By the same token, I question the purity of my love for datura. Is it really the huge, honking, white, night-blooming trumpet that attracts me, or is it the fact that every inch of this yard-tall plant, with potato-like leaves, is poisonous? "It brings on the sleep of death as quietly as fatigue does ordinary sleep, without the least struggle or motion," you wrote to Dr. Samuel Brown, describing a preparation the French made from datura during the time of Robespierre. "Every man of firmness carried it constantly in his pocket to anticipate the guillotine." It isn't my own eternal sleep I'm thinking of when I set it out in the border every year, right in a spot where the deer are wont to browse . . .

So, okay. Maybe datura doesn't count. But all the others do. All the annuals in my garden, filling the beds, spilling over borders, making hedges, rows, and drifts. All the annuals bursting out of pots and climbing up fences, and trellises, and the porch railing, and the roof. All the annuals snipped from their plants and stuck into pitchers and vases to bloom, briefly but brilliantly, from every windowsill in the kitchen and on the dining room table. All the annuals that purge March gray from my soul in glorious shades of magenta, pink, scarlet, blue, orange, and the purple of heliotrope, so royal it ought to be knighted. All the annuals that waft sweet scents, delicate fragrances, in the air, or, in the case of cleome, that just smell.

Gardening is an undiluted pleasure for me. I enjoy every

phase of it from pawing through seed catalogs to harvesting the fruit. Sowing seeds in the nursery and transplanting them in the shanty is an occupation that fills me with peace. I like preparing the beds in the spring, then planting them as May gives in to June. I like feeling the sun in my bones and clean air in my lungs, I like feeling my muscles stretch till they ache. As you asked General Henry Knox, in reference to farming, "is it not pleasanter than to be shut up within 4. walls and delving eternally with the pen?" You bet. The act of gardening repays its labors. To be able to garden is reward enough. Annuals are the bonus. The icing on the cake.

Please accept the assurance
of my great esteem and respect,

L. Simon

Dear Mr. Jefferson

If there is, every year, a documentable moment in July
when, at long last, the garden is Done, there is also, every year,
a less definable moment, usually in August, when the garden
just Is. While the former moment is based, almost exclusively,
on the physical evidence provided by empty six-packs and seed
packets, and is accompanied by exclamation points and stars on
the gardening calendar, the latter moment slips upon me so
serenely, it is often almost past before I realize it's happening.
There is no specific marker for this moment, no annual ritual to
commemorate it, no single event that brings it about. It is, in
fact, almost not a moment at all but simply a state of being that
commences at a certain time in summer and continues until a
killing frost. This year, it commenced today.

I was in the garden when I became aware of it, bending
over to pick the first two peppers of the season, sweet bells
called 'Bull Nose', which were introduced from India in 1759
and came to me from Southern Exposure Seed Exchange. Later
on, in the mellow days of September, other 'Bull Nose' will
mature to a glossy scarlet, but for now these are grass green,
and both are a little bit, charmingly, deformed. When my modern hybrids come in, orange 'Ariane' and shiny yellow
'Sunbright', they will be reliably blocky and comparatively
huge, but 'Bull Nose', synonymous with bell pepper in Fearing
Burr's *Field and Garden Vegetables of America,* is such a venera-

ble variety, it is allowed to have dented corners and an occasional sucked-in side.

Had you grown bell peppers, they probably would have been 'Bull Nose' (and, in fact, there were some in the garden when I visited Monticello last fall), but you made no reference to this kind of capsicum, only to a variety you called 'Techas' (which we would now call 'Texas'), because it was sent to you by a friend from Natchez, then part of Mexico. Although Dr. Samuel Brown did not apply any fiery adjectives in the description of their flavor, I am led to conclude, by his directions for the gingerly use of these "aromatic" peppers and by his reports of their salubrious effects on the alimentary canal, that they packed a punch. No one talks that way about bells. Indeed, bell peppers don't get much press at all.

I like them, though, and think there is no finer companion for grilled sausages than *peperonata,* a stew of peppers and onions slowly cooked in olive oil. With maybe a tomato. But it is still early times for *peperonata,* which requires more than two smallish, sweet capsicums if there is going to be enough to make it worth the trouble of cooking.

Anyway, I had an even more glorious fate in mind for these first two 'Bull Nose' as I nestled them into the picking basket, a basket, incidentally, that Jack is completely persuaded belongs to him. Then again, he thinks that about every basket, bag, and box in his range, once even climbing into the long, flat asparagus basket while I was in the garden filling it with just-cut spears. It was at that point that I had to lay down a few basic rules, which is why the two 'Bull Nose' came to rest not against a large gray cat but against seven 'Roma' tomatoes and a bouquet of basil, the seeds for which were brought to me by a friend who lives for some months of the year in Tuscany.

On the subject of Italy, I should tell you that I have been growing plum tomatoes to make pasta sauce for as long as I've been gardening, that, in fact, it was the absence of fresh plum tomatoes in American markets, after my years in Italy, that prompted me to start gardening in the first place. Ever the conscientious (repatriated) ex-patriot, the plum tomatoes I sought out and grew were 'San Marzano', a variety long considered super-*buonissimo* by the Italians. Of course, once I got the hang of gardening, I couldn't resist trying other varieties, though only as an adjunct to a full crop of 'San Marzano'.

I might add that, initially at any rate, there weren't a whole lot of other varieties to try. Seeds of plum tomatoes were just an iota less scarce in America than the plum tomatoes themselves. Happily, this sorry state soon improved due to both the gardening Renaissance and the globalization of American taste buds I've told you about, so I'm not going to go into all that again.

Sometime in the early eighties, the 1980s, that is, 'Roma' was given a trial in the garden and joined the permanent plum-tomato roster, on the spot. It wasn't a case of wild love at first taste, however, mostly, I must confess, because of my own hauteur. Despite its Italian name, 'Roma' didn't sound as authentic as 'San Marzano' to me. It seemed too obviously "Italiano" to be trusted. Besides, every catalog carried them. They were common. On the other hand, I had to grudgingly acknowledge that 'Roma' produced bushels and bushels of nice-sized, perfectly ripe, red fruits that when sliced open never revealed, as 'San Marzano' too frequently did, a black and vile-smelling core. And, okay. They didn't taste terrible, either.

That was how things stood until a few years ago when, on a summer evening, we had a tomato taste-off. I made four separate sauces with four different varieties of plums, though I prepared each one exactly the same way. Peeled and chopped tomatoes were melted down in a hot pan and seasoned, at the very end, with a tiny dice of garlic, a chiffonade of basil, and salt. Simplicity itself, and served over the most unobtrusive pasta I could think of, No. 4 spaghetti. I wanted no distractions on our tomato quest.

When the four big bowls came, steaming, to the table, the judges for this august August event—Susan, Gillie (a fellow catering friend), Jimmy, and I—dug in. 'Viva Italia', a newish hybrid, and 'San Remo', imported from Bologna, the kitchen of Italy, didn't make the first cut. It was immediately apparent that they both lacked depth. That left 'San Marzano' and 'Roma', my two stalwart varieties, locked in a duel for tomato sauce supremacy. We ate seriously, considered carefully, and interposed tastes with sips of wine. Pushing back, at last, every strand of spaghetti consumed, we rendered our final verdict. It was unanimous. An upset victory. 'Roma' was the winner. Its flavor was fuller, sweet without being cloying, and wonderfully fresh, neither pasty nor weak.

I was in shock. Ubiquitous 'Roma' was the best? Not some nearly extinct heirloom variety? Not a tomato grown for centuries in only one remote village in the mountains of Sicily? 'Roma'? Truth be told, I am still astonished, and although I've accepted, graciously I trust, the scientific truth, although 'San Marzano' has all but disappeared from the garden and 'Roma' has become the standard that replaced it, I continue to try different varieties every year, secretly hoping something better yet will come along, preferably something rare and unique. So far it hasn't.

I have had more success, on that front, in the regular tomato department. You know, with the tomatoes that you slice into slabs and drizzle with olive oil as a salad, or stack onto toast for summer breakfast, instead of smearing it with honey or jam. It was in 1993, I think, when I discovered 'Brandywine', exactly one hundred and eight years after it was first introduced, and two or three years before it became the most popular heirloom in modern commerce.

There is an excellent explanation for this sudden celebrity, of course. 'Brandywine', late-maturing, low-yielding, and ripening to a dubious pink instead of a robust red, is, nonetheless, ambrosially good. It is the quintessential tomato, the one I dream about for ten winter months. First bite to last, and there are a lot of juicy bites in each huge, misshapen fruit, 'Brandywine' is, simply put, exceptional.

Not that 'Jet Star', my mainstay, is so shabby, especially when 'Brandywine' is removed from the equation. It goes down with the utmost pleasure, pure tomato flavor that is a joy to eat and, best yet, easy to eat plenty of. It took me more years than I care to confess to realize why that was. After the millionth reading of the Harris catalog, it dawned on me that 'Jet Star' is particularly low in acid, that substance that grabs me in the back of the throat and lets my mouth know it's time to stop.

But perhaps this low acidity is why 'Jet Star' isn't overly popular, why it is harder to track down a few 'Jet Star' seeds than it is to come up with a packet of 'Brandywine'. Perhaps people associate that acid bite with the total tomato experience, though my middle-aged alimentary canal is profoundly grateful for its absence. Granted, the low acidity level makes 'Jet Star' slightly trickier to can, but I never can tomatoes anyway, I freeze them. In late August and September, giant kettles of 'Jet Star' sit on the stove all day, slowly, slowly reducing to a rich, thick pulp. When taken from the freezer, even as late as the following April or May, it makes a sauce for pizza that can't be beat.

It's always possible, of course, that the modest popularity of 'Jet Star' may just be due to the tick of time. With over five hundred varieties of tomatoes currently in existence, and more being introduced every year, it is inevitable that some of the older ones will fall by the wayside as the public's fancy is captivated by something new. I wish I could take measures to prevent the potential disappearance of 'Jet Star', that I could safeguard it, indefinitely, by propagation, as I have done with my favorite 'Fairfax' strawberry, but, alas, 'Jet Star' is a hybrid, a laboratory formula, so I am helpless to preserve it for posterity.

Certainly, this sort of tomato predicament is not one that you ever found yourself in. Although I now know that early America's fear and loathing of tomatoes has been greatly exaggerated, I think it's also fair to say that *Lycopersicon esculentum* was hardly the garden star it is today, never mind five hundred varieties of it vying for attention. By the mid-nineteenth century, when Fearing Burr discoursed on garden vegetables, he listed all twenty-four varieties then known, a quantum leap forward from the differentiation you and your contemporaries made for tomatoes, which, essentially, was none. In your Garden Book they were "tomatas," occasionally designated further as "spanish" or "dwarf," but until the 1830s that was as precise as tomato description got.

Tomato seeds were available, though, for anyone who cared to grow them, and while it required some determination to search them out, as near as I can tell, in the days before mail-order catalogs, so did everything else. David Landreth had them in Philadelphia, in the 1790s, and Grant Thorburn offered them for sale, in New York, by 1807. Bernard M'Mahon advertised them, too, although he called them "love apples" and listed them not with the vegetables but under the heading of "Physical Herbs," just below Flax and above Marsh Mallow, Pimpernel, and Rue.

In his *American Gardener's Calendar*, M'Mahon seemed to have a clearer sense of them when he advised his readers that "the Capsicums, Tomatoes, and Eggplants, being in much estimation for culinary purposes," should be sown in hotbeds in March and planted out in the garden "as early . . . as the night frosts shall have totally disappeared." I know he was trying to inform and encourage a skeptical audience about a trio of garden crops that was both unfamiliar and suspect, which is why I find it ironic that it is this very threesome that I have come to consider The Jewels in the Crown, the summer highlight of the kitchen garden. In fact, having plucked the two 'Bull Nose' peppers from their sturdy bushes and settled them into Jack's basket alongside the 'Roma' tomatoes, I was headed for the eggplant next.

My choice tonight was 'Ichiban', one of the skinny, purple Oriental types. About eight inches long, and only a fraction bigger around than a banana, I thought it was stunted the first time I grew it. This was not a wholly unreasonable conclusion to draw, since it rained in early June that year, and then not again until August 6th. There were a lot of miniature vegetables that summer, although I now realize that 'Ichiban' wasn't one of them. It's supposed to be that size. And as such, it could be what the adage makers had in mind when they decided that good things come in small packages, because 'Ichiban' is the best eggplant I've eaten to date.

I came to eggplant eating late in life, probably no more than a decade ago. Before that, try as I might, I could barely bring myself to swallow it. Unless it was cooked to a dehydrated crisp, there was something about eggplant that made me decidedly queasy. This despite my long, all-embracing residence in Italy, where eggplant has been savored for several centuries at least. Somewhat defensively, I feel compelled to add that, except for the Spaniards, no one else in Europe, or in the colonies, seemed to share this enthusiasm. Not until the nineteenth century was well under way, in any event. Even then, it wasn't overwhelmingly popular, and, unlike the tomato, which got off to an equally shaky start, eggplant never achieved the unequivocal acceptance of its more famous Solanaceae cousin.

I have a few theories about why this is, theories based solely on conjecture and personal experience. My conversion came the year Burpee sent me a bonus packet of their hybrid eggplant seeds, and I decided, what the heck, I might as well plant them. I couldn't resist growing something I never had before, and if worst came to worst, I could send the purple blimps, UPS, to Susan, who has always enjoyed them. When a couple of shiny, round fruits finally seemed perfectly ripe, I cut them up and cooked them. And passed into a new gastronomic era. They were fantastic. Hence theory number one: Eggplant is one of those vegetables, like brussels sprouts and cauliflower, that is inedible unless it is garden-grown, in which instance it is delicious.

In the years since my eggplant rapprochement, I have attempted, carefully, judiciously, to eat eggplant I didn't grow. With one or two exceptions that I'll get to in theory number three, these trials have been close to disastrous. Mal de mer all over again. So theory number two: Eggplant has to be eaten either absolutely fresh or else by a truer devotee than me.

Although I have no hard data to prove it, I unswervingly believe that there's something going on behind that gleaming purple skin, some eggplant sorcery, an enzymatic process, perhaps, that commences the minute the fruit is picked. The longer it sits, severed, the more this process accelerates, reverting the delectable, almost nutty-flavored flesh to its bitter and nasty Asian origins. And why not? After all, we know that corn starts losing its sugar shortly after being snapped from the stalk, so why shouldn't eggplant similarly deteriorate upon being snipped from the plant?

Theory number three revolves around methods of cooking, and, simply stated, goes: The gustatory satisfaction derived from eggplant is directly proportional to its chosen preparation as a meal. For my money, in the case of eggplant without provenance, this means slicing it fairly thin, then either searing it on the grill or roasting it in the oven. There is something about cooking it this way that renders the questionable eggplant highly palatable, and renders the garden-grown and freshly picked ones delicious beyond imagining. Maybe it's because whatever ill-flavored essences are lurking in the spongy interior get cooked away instead of getting saturated with either sauce or fat, magnifying the unwelcome effect. Whatever the reason, I've noticed that this theory also holds true for bluefish, another staple of summer, and, coincidentally, a splendid condiment for eggplant.

Fortunately, this third theory did not have to be invoked today because my harvest went straight from the garden to the chopping block with no more than ten minutes passing before the eggplant hit the pan. I don't know whether or not you belonged to the eggplant-pressing school (Mary Randolph recommended parboiling eggplant to "take off the bitter taste"), but contemporary culinary advice calls for salting the sliced or diced fruit, then pressing it under a weighted pie plate to make the bitter taste run off as juice. I always followed these instructions to the letter until the day I realized that 'Ichiban', though I squeezed it for all it was worth, never managed to produce more than a meager drop of liquid, barely brown with bitterness, so I promptly abandoned the practice. There are those who will tell you that this lack of bitterness is due to modern breeding, and others who swear that it is a characteristic of the Oriental varieties. Still others claim that the heirloom Italian eggplants are incomparable, a claim that sounds tailor-made for me, and one I mean to test starting next year.

For the moment, though, only the tomatoes and the basil are Italian. The eggplant is Japanese, the peppers came from India, and the onions, already in the kitchen, are 'Copra,' a hybrid from America, not the Seychelles, a story I never did get around to telling you. Tonight we'll eat them, cooked together with a 'Thai Hot' pepper and a mammoth clove of 'German Extra Hardy' garlic, in a French dish called ratatouille, which has recently devolved into something of a cliché, an unfortunate turn of events, because when made with garden-fresh ingredients, it is so good tears of happiness run down my cheeks.

Ratatouille, for me, is summer. It is tomatoes, peppers, and eggplant, The Jewels in the Crown, the fine fruits of long, hot, sun-filled days. Aromatic of basil, its flavors are melded together, the way an August afternoon becomes an indolent fusion of tempering light, blue sky, and heat. I don't know if it is truly ratatouille that I make, if it is the authentic French version, because I am not in the habit of adhering to recipes, unless they are my sister's or unless I am baking. Instead, I go into the garden and see what is ripe and tempting, which I'm sure is how ratatouille got invented in the first place. It suggests itself, on a midsummer day, tucked amongst their foliage, bright and shiny tomatoes, peppers, and eggplant, beckoning the cook.

I'll bet it was the thought of ratatouille, as I bent to pick those first two 'Bull Nose', that triggered this year's realization that the garden finally Is. It is finally a garden, twenty-seven full, lush beds' worth, not a sparse patchwork, a loose collection of seedlings, strings, and hope. Sometime, unbeknownst, it crossed over that ephemeral line, no longer a shimmering vision in my mind, an anonymous Eden, but a real garden, alive with real textures, tastes, colors, and smells.

Maybe because of my work and my plans, or maybe despite them, it has its own character, distinct from all the gardens that preceded it. It's a character wrought by an incalculable combination of sunshine and rain, by temperatures rising and falling, by how deep the frost was last winter, and what grew in the soil last summer. It has been wrought by an arcane equation of science and luck. For better or worse, though, this year's garden is now an established fact, it is set on its inalterable course, finally being the garden I intended, as amended by Nature.

I don't mean to mislead you. Everything in the garden is not at the peak of its bloom. Far from it. Sure, the tomatoes, peppers, and eggplants are starting to produce in abundance, but while The Jewels in the Crown may be symbolic of summer—all right, even gluttonously good—they are not the whole show. The peas, for example, those tiny, sweet petits pois, are over and done with, and, I might add, were a great disappointment.

They had troubles, this year, right from the start. The ground was too soggy, I think, and their germination was poor.

Then June was even windier than usual, and the young sur-vivors got thrashed about as they gripped, with their corkscrew pea tendrils, the trellis behind them. July came in with a rush of heat, blasting them almost overnight from ridiculously small even for petits pois to woody and coarse.

The strawberries, on the other hand, basked in that hot sun, taking advantage of the opportunity to turn spectacularly juicy and sweet. Most of them, as usual, were eaten *in situ*, though a few of the berries made it into the freezer, where they'll cool their heels until Christmas when Jimmy makes his crepes. They are also over and done with now, mowed down to the nub, in fact, mulched with manure, and already making new leaves.

The same goes for the asparagus, except that it, instead of being cut to the quick, has been left to its own devices and has made, as usual, ferns seven feet high. I had to put in an emer-gency call to Dede to please tie them up, because she was the only one who remembered exactly how many lengths of clothesline got strung between fence posts to corral the tall, frothy foliage. Despite being a schoolteacher these days, she came to the rescue. As a bonus, for old time's sake, Hilary checked behind the cold frame, free of charge, to make sure there were no rabbits menacing us.

In addition to the crops that are completely past, just a memory, a note on the calendar, there are those that have yet to make their mark, those that are barely begun. Just cresting the surface in the bed where the peas made their valiant stand, in vain, are the shoots of haricots verts, two double rows of the century-old 'Triumph de Farcy'. At the moment they look lost and scared, tiny humped-over green stems in a naked rectangle of soil, but by the end of September, they'll fill the whole bed with their squat bushes and wide leaves, slender, tender beans dangling, tantalizingly, beneath them. That is, they will barring hail, hurricanes, or a break in the fence, allowing in an invasion of rabbits or deer. We can easily fend off an early frost, as long as we know it's coming, by throwing a tarp over the bed after dinner and taking it off before breakfast. The beans actually are crunchier with that extra chill.

The cole crops and the fall fennel haven't gotten even as far as the garden, never mind into their designated bed. For that matter, their bed isn't made yet, since the onions were there first, and they aren't ready to relinquish it. But almost. They've given up growing and their once rakish green tops, now a sickly yellow, are fainting in the aisles. We'll be pulling them any day soon. In the meantime, round two is waiting in the cold frame, having been transplanted into four-packs only last week.

There are three kinds of kale this year. The two varieties I usually grow, sweet, mauve-stemmed 'Red Russian' and the traditional 'Dwarf Blue Curled Scotch', are both old enough to have been at Monticello, and, in fact, 'Red Russian' was. And if it wasn't 'Dwarf Blue Curled Scotch' that you also sowed, it was a very close Scotch cousin. It could be that you grew my new addition, too, though perhaps with a different name. I've got a pair of four-packs of "Wild Garden Kale" coming along, which Shepherd's Garden Seeds swears is not only colorful to behold, it's also tasty to eat. It is unclear, however, whether the "Wild" refers to the kale's origin or to its appearance.

There are three broccolis as well this year, although one of these *is* in the garden, and has been since June. It's called 'Minaret', and because it takes more than a hundred days to mature, I give it an early start. This is a broccoli worth waiting for, though, first because it looks like a fantasy spaceship about to lift off, and then because of its marvelous flavor that has an aftermath of nuts. 'Minaret' is planted next to the brussels sprouts, set out on the same day in June, because they, like the Romanesque-type broccoli, need a long season before they are ready to harvest. Together they promise to make a vivid show, as the heads of 'Minaret', spiraling madly to a point, are a bright chartreuse, while one of the brussels sprouts, 'Red Rubine', is reputed to make burgundy-purple-hued sprouts. So far neither of these brassicas has shown its unusual colors, but the plants are looking healthy and sturdy, knock wood.

If we're talking about color, though, apart from the flowers, I'll tell you what ready-to-eat, riotous spectacle is currently attracting attention. It's the chard row. Leading off is a variety called 'Charlotte', which I picked out of the Pinetree catalog because it has the same name as a friend, Charlotte Maison, the director of the Nantucket Atheneum. The moral is that friendship pays, because 'Charlotte' the chard is a gorgeous, glossy garnet with a nice, mild taste. When cooked and tossed into rice, with toasted pine nuts, goat cheese, and chives, it not only makes a fresh summer dish, it turns the whole creation a startling shade of pink.

Next down the row is 'Vulcan', a variety that in any other circumstance would be the star, but in this setting, its deep, intensely green leaves and scarlet red stems are merely the warm-up for the chard that grows beyond it. 'Joseph's Coat', as its name suggests, is a pageant. It's stalks, tall, proud masts for the variously wrinkled, crumpled, and nearly smooth banners of leaves, are not only familiar red or white but also orange, yellow, or pink.

Shepherd's says that 'Joseph's Coat' is an heirloom from Australia, which somehow seems right, because even though

I've never been Down Under, I have the sense that it is a land of vibrant hues and extraordinary sights. You remember Australia, don't you? It's that continent on the other side of the world where England sent all the malcontents and miscreants when America stopped being available. It might interest you to know that Australia has also turned out remarkably well, quite a success story, and in more ways than chard.

Mixing chard and rice in a salad, shocking pink or standard-issue white, is just one variation on a culinary theme that has no limits that I know of. I love combining vegetables and rice, and, without meaning to boast, the dishes that result, more often than not, range anywhere from pretty damn good to really great. Dear Jimmy is so taken by them, he keeps saying I ought to write a rice-salad cookbook, but as gratifying as it is to have an appreciative audience, I think I'll leave cookbooks to Susan.

Besides, all my recipes would be boringly similar. Find the best variety, grow it in good soil, and harvest it moments before cooking. A foolproof formula. "The true cookery is to deal only with the best and tenderest of each kind, and jealously preserve its flavour," William Robinson, of landscape fame, wrote about vegetables in 1885. "Old or inferior vegetables require the coarser devices of the cook, and must be saturated with grease and spices to make them edible."

While I wholeheartedly agree with his former point, and go along, guardedly, with his latter, I hope my fundamental approach to cooking vegetables is not quite so relentlessly ascetic. Certainly, I have never been an advocate of "old or inferior" vegetables, but I am all in favor of a few discreet herbs, and, as you yourself said, olive oil renders "an infinitude of vegetables . . . a proper and comfortable nourishment." Then again, I told you William Robinson could be a curmudgeon. A man of decided opinions, to say the least. Knowing your fondness for French cuisine, I don't dare repeat the disdainful remarks he reserves for French chefs, "supposed to be the best," who drown all their "delicate" vegetables in an ocean of butter.

I don't take a hard line on butter, either. There are some vegetables it complements nicely. A baked potato, for example, is its natural foil, and what about an ear of corn? I know that the corn you grew was mostly for hominy or meal, a normal enough practice in your day. Although sweet corn has been around since Columbus "discovered" America, none of the new population paid it much mind, until breeders got their hands on it in the second half of the nineteenth century. Today one of the rituals of summer is a feed of corn on the cob, ideally swiped, piping hot, across a bar of butter, and then given a sprinkle of salt. Personally, I can't face the prospect of winter without having had piles of 'Sweet Sue' and 'Silver Queen' at regular and frequent intervals throughout the preceding summer.

Despite my sweet-corn dependence, I must tell you that this is the one garden vegetable I *don't* grow. Unless you count okra, which I don't have the courage to eat, or the several seasons I declared the garden a zucchini-free zone. But sweet corn is particular, and requires regular and repeated sowings, as well as regular and vigilant pickings, in order to keep up with that regular and frequent schedule of meals. The real reason I don't bother to grow corn, though, is because Steve Slosek does, down the road at Moor's End Farm, and as I once told you, it's the best sweet corn I've ever had. Moreover, Steve picks it at the precisely perfect moment, and it is so tender and juicy, swiping it in butter is like gilding the lily. Especially the next day for lunch. All things considered, Steve's corn is hard to top.

I do grow popcorn, however. Unlike sweet corn, I can sow it in June, then leave it alone until it is dry and rustly in October. This year, as most, it's planted in hills down the center of the squash bed, standing tall above the 'Blue' hubbard, the 'Waltham' butternut, and the new 'Tuffy' acorn. This is my tribute to the traditional Iroquois Three Sisters–system of crops, except that the third member of this triad, the beans, aren't climbing up the cornstalks but are climbing up poles between the brussels sprouts and 'Minaret' broccoli instead.

I've noticed that ears of popcorn are starting to form, and that one or two butternut squash are turning from green to tan. The 'Purple Peacock' pole beans are about ready to pick, though the 'King of the Garden' limas need another few weeks. Over in the salad bed, we're working on the fourth set of lettuces, and the 'Red Stalk' celery, an heirloom from England, is beginning to look like celery instead of some kind of mutant parsley. The 'Gladiator' parsnips have luxuriant, green tops, with crisp, broad leaves, as opposed to the luxuriant, ferny tops of the 'Lindoro' carrots that are their neighbor. And in the row after that, 'Laura' leeks are as big around as Laura thumbs.

Seven kinds of shelling beans are slowly swelling in their pods, getting plumper and meatier in preparation for next winter's soups and stews. 'Fowler' bush beans, another heirloom, though this one from Oregon, are waiting to be plucked, dashed for the smallest instant into boiling water, and eaten with a few leaves of arugula. Dressed with olive oil and a grind of black pepper. Are you listening, William Robinson?

The eggplant is gleaming, the peppers have commenced, and when I walk by the 'Sweet 100' cherry tomatoes, they practically pop into my mouth for a snack. The blueberries are finished, but I ate the first raspberry yesterday, and by the end of the month, I'll be eating them by the fistful. We've been seething new potatoes since the middle of July, especially the heavenly fingerlings, 'Nosebag' and 'La Reine'. And everywhere I look there are flowers. What else could this be but a garden?

It is ten months of escalating toil, beginning with the map last October, and culminating with tilling, raking, planting, and now the never-ending hoeing. It is ten months of agonizing and organizing, ten months of anticipation, laying tiny flecks of seeds on their pillows of soil and imagining this day in August when they are a brilliant bouquet on the kitchen windowsill or ratatouille simmering in a pot on the stove. It is a garden.

Even more than the sum of vegetables and flowers, though, more than the mouthwatering meals, more than the roasted asparagus spears, or haricots verts and arugula, more than the big rose-colored trumpets of *Cobaea* climbing up the cucumber trellis with the crisp fruits of 'Sweet Success', more than the juice of 'Fairfax' strawberries dribbling down my chin or the pungent juice of 'Copra' onions making tears slide down my face, more than pulling carrots from underneath the snow, more than the welcoming daffodils when they announce that it's spring, more than the ten months of making, more than a goal achieved, a function fulfilled, more than that, this garden is part of me.

Better still, it is part of every garden that has been, both the ones in this potato-shaped spot and others all over the world. It owes a debt to every traditional kitchen garden laid out along paths and in beds, and to every kitchen gardener who created the tradition by doing so, and who, by doing so, kept the tradition alive. It reflects that tradition as transformed by America's natives, who offered vegetable seeds and gardening wisdom to the European colonists wading up on their shores. Where would the Three Sisters bed be, otherwise?

This garden is part of Victorian follies and the tulip madness that overtook seventeenth-century Holland. Part of Kansas cornfields, with ruler-straight rows, and English cottages, with overstuffed yards. It wouldn't be this garden without seed catalogs, without James L. Vick and Joseph Harris. Without David Landreth's three hundred and seventy-five Bloomsdale acres and W. Atlee Burpee's Fordhook Farm. Without Rob Johnston at Johnny's Selected Seeds or the Ronnigers and their sixty inches of soil.

Over in that row, some plum tomatoes are ripening, grown from seeds sent to me last fall from a farm in Sicily. Maybe I'll finally have the rare, wonderful sauce I've been yearning for. I'll know in less than a week. In a neighboring bed is the hubbard squash, brought to Marblehead, Massachusetts, by a sea captain in 1798 or, another version goes, in 1820. Whatever the date, it was through the efforts of Mrs. Elizabeth Hubbard that it found its way into commerce and is, two hundred years later, sprawled out in my garden next to 'Tuffy', newly bred and introduced only this season.

It took ten months to arrive at this moment, this moment when it all came together, but those ten months stretch back untold centuries and reach into the unknown future. Not just the sum of its vegetables and flowers, this garden is a thread of life. It connects me to the colonial Australians, who liked their chard flamboyant, and to the ancestors of Don Fowler's friend in Oregon, who probably didn't eat their bush beans with olive oil and arugula. Best of all, it connects me to Monticello, through 'Tennis Ball' lettuce and the fabulous, fairy clarion

Mirabilis. But in one of those turns that make life so provocative, it also connects me to gardens that have yet to be planted.

"I am still devoted to the garden," you wrote in your sixty-eighth year. "But though an old man, I am but a young gardener." Mr. Jefferson, we are all young gardeners. Gardeners are ageless and the gardens we create go on forever.

Please accept the assurance
of my great esteem and respect,

L. Simon

The Jewels in the Crown
and Jack